Praise

Falling In Love
An Unlikely Tale of Happily Ever After

Falling in Love Backwards is a profound testament to the power of telling the truth, listening to your heart (even when your mind doesn't agree), and bravely stepping into your future. With rare and raw courage, the authors give you a road map to real intimacy, with honesty and grace. Bravo to Landon and Diane, who were willing to bare their souls with the intention of supporting others in their quest for love.

I love this book and highly recommend it.

— *Denise Linn, best selling author of* Sacred Space

Landon Carter and Diane Covington-Carter have written a book that tells the truth, that powerfully describes what it really takes to make a relationship work.

I recommend this remarkable book and the account of their extraordinary love affair to anyone who longs for a relationship that is mutually empowering, respectful, honest, and truly transformational. Falling in Love Backwards is a courageous and beautiful saga that will lift your heart, open your mind, and nourish your soul.

— *Lynne Twist, author of* The Soul of Money

Amazing, compelling, gripping—I couldn't stop reading. I appreciated the rawness of it and how you had to get out of your head and listen to your heart. Such a testimony of the true meaning of courage, the root of which is 'heart'.

Carol Nimick, Teacher, California

Praise for *Falling in Love Backwards*

I stayed up 'til 3am last night reading...transfixed. I cannot emphasize enough how VALUABLE this material is. Our society needs the benefit of this information.

I don't know anyone willing to go "to any length" the way you two have done to break through in the area of relationship. To be able to stand on your shoulders and reap the benefits of all your hard work is priceless.

I began reading the book, absolutely knowing that I did not have a clue and now, I have more insight than I ever knew was possible. I am forever indebted to you & Landon for clearing away the brush and creating this path. I salute your courage, your bravery and your amazing fortitude in seeing this through. I see that, contrary to my previous belief, I am completely able, willing and ready to embark upon this journey!

THANK YOU, you brave & beautiful beings!

Jane Press, Teacher, Playwright & Actress, California

This book is a template of love, for everyone to learn how to go to the deeper place, how to know 'this is a yes' and to stay with that through the storms. For all relationships, that is the work to be done. It was really powerful to have the male and female points of view and perspectives. Just marvelous. I was blown away.

Jeanette Piety, Investment Wizard, California

Praise for *Falling in Love Backwards*

I am inspired and deeply admire your courage, dedication and true Spirit.

Val Jon Farris, Consultant, California

Landon and Diane have fanned the embers of "Being Met" into the deep fire of a "Soul Love". I found the book exhilarating, intriguing, hope filled and beautiful.

Zena Whitcombe, Healer, California

I just finished your book and I loved it! I really enjoyed reading the two perspectives...that made it very interesting and unique. I found myself wanting to read more and curious how it was all going to work out, even though I already knew the ending. It was a page- turner!

Heather Williams, CEO, Gratitude Organics

Oh My God! This book was so moving. Phenomenal. It's real, authentic and powerful. A must read for the planet. Incredibly Strong. I've never seen anything like it.

Mardi Boone, Business Owner, Canada

I'm in awe of who you both are. The book describes EXACTLY what I'm up to—not settling for anything less than extraordinary, yet feeling like sometimes it's hopeless. The book gives me HOPE!!! It just feels good.

Micole Noble, Mindfulness Coach, California

Falling in love BACKWARDS

An unlikely tale of

Happily Ever After

Diane Covington-Carter

Landon Carter

Falling in Love BACKWARDS
An Unlikely Tale of Happily Ever After

Published by CarterCovington
12072 Willow Valley Road, Nevada City, CA 95959

Second Edition

This book is set in Cambria Type Text.
Printed in the United States of America

First Edition: January 2013
Second Edition: October 2013

ISBN-10: 0991044614
ISBN-13: 978-0-9910446-1-0

DEDICATION

To our parents, who did their best to teach us about love.

To all of our teachers, known and unknown, whose many contributions brought us to where this love story begins.

And finally, to you, our readers, who know in your hearts that true love exists and that a more loving world is possible.

ACKNOWLEDGMENTS

We'd especially like to thank our generous friends and
family, who read over our drafts and helped us to clarify our
message: Bill Carter, Val Jon Farris, Denise Linn, Cheryl Murray,
Micole Noble, Jeanette Piety, Jane Press, Susan Prilliman, and
Heather Williams. Their encouragement and enthusiasm made
a huge difference in bringing the book into reality.

Back cover wedding day photo of Diane and Landon by
Georgette Aronow Photography, Nevada City, California. Cover
photo by Cheryl Reed-Dudley of Moscow, Idaho. Book layout
and cover design by Margaret Jean Campbell, Nevada City,
California.

CONTENTS

"Being deeply loved by someone gives you strength,

While loving someone deeply gives you courage."

~ Lao Tzu ~

6th century BCE

Diane's Prologue

Words evoke images and feelings and transport us to other worlds. I discovered this as a child, when I'd pour over my thick, worn *Grimm's Fairy Tales* book. I'd curl up for as many hours as I could steal from chores and hot summer days and read and reread my favorites—Cinderella, the Frog Prince and Twelve Dancing Princesses. At the end, things all turned out and they lived "happily ever after." Wow, could that be possible?

I grew up in the 1950's, part of the 78 million post World War II "baby boom," during a peaceful, prosperous and even innocent time in America.

But as I looked around in my young life, I didn't see much "happily ever after," especially between my parents. The one time I remember seeing my father try to hug my mother, she pushed him away. She modeled how to treat a man by a seething silence or an outright cutting remark, both painful to watch.

I adored my dad, whose sparkly blue eyes shone with warmth and love. Dad grew up on a farm in South Dakota and put himself through college to become an engineer. He had a simple and down to earth approach to life and loved being a father. My mother, on the other hand, grew up spoiled and rich in Melbourne, Australia. Her father had deserted the family when she was a toddler and though her rich grandfather took care of them, she grew up without a father. She also grew up under the shadow of a lie about what had really happened—they told her that her father had died.

My mother's cold and critical manner expressed the jealousy she felt about my close and healthy relationship with my father and she took it out on me with physical and emotional abuse.

Because of the conflicting messages from my parents and all the tension between them, I felt sad, confused and frightened. I bit my fingernails down to the quick and fell asleep each night terrified of the boogie man. I grew up convinced that I was not good enough, even though my father loved and encouraged me. My mother's venom won out.

In the midst of this, my sister Sharon, just two years older than me, accepted and loved me. Early on we must have figured out it was much more fun to play than to fight and we adored each other. I know that I laughed more with Sharon than any other person in my life. She also shielded me some from my mother's anger.

When I started school, I longed to find the "answers" in life, to happiness and love, to "happily ever after." I saw happy people in movies and on television, so there had to be a way out of the cloud of fear I lived under and the unhappiness I saw my parents acting out.

Each year, I would begin school hopeful— maybe this year they would talk about the *important* things in life, the things I longed to learn—how to be happy, how to love, how to solve arguments. And why were there starving children in China or why did we kill other people in wars—it all didn't make sense to me. But each year, my hopes would fade unfulfilled. I loved learning and school, but why was no one talking about the really *important* questions?

My parents split up when I, the youngest, left for college at seventeen. Confused and upset about that change in my young life, I signed up for psychology classes, eager to learn how to unravel my inner turmoil. I studied Freud and Jung's interesting theories and tried to apply them to my own personal challenges. It seemed that if I wanted to get some help, it would take ten years on a psychoanalyst's couch to begin to heal.

I also learned about rats and mazes, something called "intermittent reinforcement" and other facts that garnered A's on multiple-choice exams but which left me wondering how this could all help me to feel happier. Though I graduated with honors, I left feeling "there are no true answers here" on my search for happily ever after.

I married young—nineteen, hoping to find happiness in marriage and motherhood. But the model of relationship my parents had acted out hung over my life like a black cloud. My young husband and I had no communication skills to deal with the challenges of life and parenthood in our twenties.

I continued my search, going to therapy, taking a powerful journal writing class created by a psychoanalyst, and reading every self help and new age book I could find. In one book, I read about the *est* training, which promised that you could "change your life in two weekends"—an outrageous claim in the late 1970's.

I found my way to the *est* training when I was twenty-eight and loved it—I did feel like I changed my life in two weekends. I took on the concepts of taking responsibility for my life and happiness, of stopping being right and making other people wrong and many other powerful and useful tools. I also found a community of people, where we could be authentic and genuine about our lives, rather than pretending to "have it all together."

Est offered an advanced program called the *Six-Day Course*, created by a trainer named Landon Carter. The course involved jumping off a mountain on a zip-line, rappelling down a cliff and pulling yourself across a canyon with two ropes, among other terrifying things.

I still carried a lot of fear inside and signed up hoping to have a breakthrough in my life. In the months, weeks and days leading up to the course, I felt shivers of terror each time I thought about what I had signed up for. But I also felt a thrill of excitement that if other people could overcome their fears and do that course, then I could too.

At the *Six-Day Course*, I stood on the edge of the cliff, harnessed into the zip-line and looked out over the expanse below. My stomach clenched tight and my mind screamed that "now, for sure, you are going to die." But I was aware of something else inside, a quiet place that felt calm and good. I trusted that new space and stepped off.

I whizzed through the air, whooping and hollering, swinging my arms and legs, and screaming in delight all the way down to the bottom. What a thrill! I discovered that I could be so much bigger than my thoughts and fears.

Besides the ropes events, the course challenged us every moment of the other five days. Each day began at six, with exercise and jogging and ended in the early hours of the next morning, after we'd been looking at our lives from every possible angle.

We faced our bodies, in a bathing suit process, our beliefs about our sexuality, our deep personal fears and wounds.

At the beginning of the course, we'd all been videotaped, introducing ourselves. Then, day-by-day, Landon went over each of the one hundred videos, working with people to let go of their "acts."

Participants revealed things they'd never talked about before and in the powerful space, we all felt freer and more willing to take risks in life and to stop hiding out. Those six-days impacted and changed the course of my life.

The trainer for the course impressed me. He had gone to ivy-league schools and been successful, but then went off to India to sit with a guru named Sai Baba for eight months. When he returned, after taking the *est* training, he became a trainer. It was a revelation to see a man who was intelligent, well educated and classy and who had devoted his life to waking up and to helping others to discover who they really were.

There had been one moment on my way up to the ropes course and zip line, when he'd been walking around observing and he stopped by our group. I looked at him and he turned and looked at me. Just for those few seconds, he seemed so present and I felt truly seen. I also saw his goodness. He was married and I was married, but in my heart, I tucked away those moments and labeled him as my "ideal man."

But he also intimidated me. By the time he got to my video, at the end of the course, when he said he didn't see much there, I shuddered in relief. I had been terrified to be under his close scrutiny.

The last day of our course, he encouraged us to "use everything you've got to make a difference in life." *He's doing that*, I thought, as I listened and thought about his words. *He's using his good looks, his intelligence and his integrity to impact our lives and the lives of thousands of others.* His words echoed in my thoughts over the coming years.

After the course, I returned home with the courage to take some much needed leaps in my personal life. My two daughters were ten and four and I loved my family, but my husband and I couldn't communicate without arguing and were at an impasse. I also faced the reality that for years I had been looking for answers to questions that he wasn't interested in asking.

I suggested that maybe if we separated, we could get some counseling, some perspective and heal our relationship. The day we discussed separating, he told a woman at work, they got together and he didn't look back.

Even with my newfound fearlessness from the *Six-Day Course*, all my fears of "not being good enough" from my childhood surfaced, I felt abandoned and went through tremendous pain. But thanks to my friends within *est*, and the courses I was taking, I got through it. On the positive side, I was thirty years old and finally free to follow my dreams of looking for answers to the deepest questions I could find.

In the years ahead, I studied with a man who taught me a powerful life coaching approach and began working with clients. In addition, I studied hypnosis, Neurolinguistic Programming and the Enneagram, traveled twice to India to sit with a master, and went to Esalen Institute for classes and seminars. I devoted my life to my own personal growth and to helping others to grow and change. Even my writing, which I loved and which began to be published, was mostly personal essays of trying to unravel the mysteries of life.

As the years passed, I experienced many successes in life—work I loved, healthy and happy daughters, great friends and good health. I traveled and even fulfilled a dream of living in France for eight months. In my forties, I moved to a small town in the Sierras to be near my sister and bought a run-down organic apple farm. As I worked to restore the farm, watering, clearing, planting, pruning, and mowing, it felt like I was also healing myself. The farm became a place of peace and solace, where I could feel my depths and listen to my soul.

But the one area that still eluded me was finding my soul mate and partner. I knew that the deep wounds with my mother were at the core of that issue and continued to work to try to heal them. I had many relationships over the years with some really good men, but none of them had "felt right" to make a long-term commitment. I vowed that I would not marry again unless I was one hundred percent sure and I never was. In almost all the cases, I ended the relationships.

In my spiritual life, I had given up on the Catholic Church, but still prayed to Saint Michael, with whom I felt a deep connection, after visiting the Abbey Mont St. Michel, in France. I found a teacher named John O'Donohue, an Irish poet, philosopher and former priest. His book *Anam Cara*, which means "soul friend" in Celtic, had a profound impact on me.

One of my favorite quotes from that book was *"you must learn, therefore, to treat yourself with great tenderness."* I had never heard anything like that before. I began to work to create a sense of tenderness within, a sense of mothering myself in a way that my mother had been unable to do.

O'Donohue also taught me that I was being "minded" or looked after and that I could trust life. In *Anam Cara*, he noted that the phrase "Do not be afraid" appears 366 times in the bible. I began to notice ways that I was being minded and began to trust more.

In 2003, when my sister Sharon died of brain tumors after a long illness, I again turned to O'Donohue's work to find solace. I attended two spiritual retreats with him and at one of them, when I mentioned my challenges with my mother, he commented: *"just be kind to her, she's old and you're not."* That became my mantra through the last years of my mother's life. I was kind to her no matter what she did. She never changed her harsh and critical behavior, but I focused on being kind anyway.

I would think, *some people go and sit on top of a mountaintop to wake up. I have this person as my mother for my training.* Before my mother died in 2007, we'd reached a peaceful place between us. I mothered her in a way that she had never been able to mother me.

I had read that the true meaning of the word "virgin" was "a woman whole unto herself." From all the work I'd done in my life and the healing with my mother, I felt more whole. After her death, I felt ready to search for my partner.

Friends encouraged me to try Internet dating, but I found it to be a dead end. I wanted to be more than a pretty face or someone to drink wine with. I was searching for a partner who had been on a spiritual path as I had been, and who shared my deep values of personal growth and of trying to unravel and heal the ways we were bound up in life.

I tried an online dating site for "spiritual singles" and a man from the east coast contacted me. After a few weeks of long phone conversations, he wanted to fly west and visit for a week. But as the visit got closer, I realized I felt uncomfortable having a week long "first date" and told him no.

Since I'd already set aside the time for his visit, I decided to create a personal retreat for myself, the first week of the New Year, 2009. Day after day, I sat by a crackling fire and wrote, meditated and read. In the quiet, deep, rich space, I listened for what my soul wanted for the New Year and for my life.

This brings you up to the point where our story begins. Our intention in sharing this very personal and transparent story is to show how we navigated the painful and difficult issues that can arise in an intimate relationship.

We hope that reading the tale of our journey creates some healing in your life, brings you joy and freedom and some steps closer to finding a deep and powerful relationship and your "happily ever after."

Love and blessings,
Diane Covington-Carter

Landon's Prologue

This book tells the story of how the things I knew to be true through insight and reasoning, taught in my seminars, and wrote about in my previous book, *Living Awake*, finally manifested in my own life. It is a tribute to my angel, Diane, without whom I would not have the wonderful life I am now living. And it is written with gratitude to all the teachers, friends, and lovers along the way who have contributed to my growth in the realm of intimate relationships.

First, a little background to this chapter in my life. My marriage to my wife of nineteen years and the mother of my children had ended in divorce some seventeen years back. I would characterize that relationship as the typical "falling in love, can't eat, can't sleep" start. She was definitely "it" for me, no questions, and not only did we grow up together, we worked hard to try and make the relationship work, and learned a lot about ourselves in the process.

But we didn't know enough to solve the fundamental problems that arose and I would say we were not working at a deep enough level. We have three great children, wonderful grand children and are friends. She is happily remarried and she and her husband recently attended Diane's and my wedding.

After our divorce, I decided to have a relationship with whomever I was attracted to, so in the years that followed, I had many serial monogamous relationships and in each I seemed to be learning a different lesson. Often times, I'd be playing the opposite role in the subsequent relationship to learn the lesson from both sides.

The lessons included abandonment, boundaries, how we processed upsets, or whether this relationship was "it" for one or the other. So it went for the next fifteen years after moving out of our family house in the Bay Area to Pagosa Springs, Colorado and finally immigrating to Golden Bay, New Zealand.

During this time, I was more and more willing to listen to my feelings about things and to trust that at least if I followed my feelings, I was being true to some aspect of myself. And I was having insights in my meditations that continued to guide me. Certain things were clear to me as I drove up Diane's driveway in the fall of 2009.

First, if you "fall in love," you are partly falling in love with your fantasies and would need tools to deal with the realities when they arose. So many relationships I had been in started on a high only to end on a low. I was determined to discover the secret to success in the challenging domain of relationship.

Second, I was committed to having both full connection with my partner and freedom to be myself. I had seen too many couples compromise one aspect for the other in a kind of dance of "draw near then push away" ending up with a diminished experience of both aspects and some resentment besides. In fact I had done that dance in my relationship with my children's mother. But I was fairly sure you could have both full connection and freedom to be yourself.

And third, I was committed to enlightenment and freedom and had been since waking up at twenty-eight in India with Satya Sai Baba. Having tried the ascetic's path I was certain that I was no celibate monk and had been advocating intimate relationships as a fast path to freedom if you could stay awake. But I had not yet been with a partner who was up to the challenge.

It is interesting that with Diane, I did not "fall in love with her" in my typical pattern. In fact I would characterize our relationship for me as "falling in love backwards." Because there was no "fantasy," we started out living in the reality of our experience and dealing with the problems that arose. Now, we have arrived at the stage where I am deeply in love with my wife, Diane. And it is the most complete, nurturing, grounding experience I have ever had in my life, for which I am enormously grateful.

This book is about the journey from what most would label as a very rough start to where we are today. It is the combination of a good romance story and a self-help book as it not only tells a story, but it also describes what we have learned through our experiences: the insights, understandings and practices that we hope will be helpful to you.

For it is my premise that there is no reason you have to spend the years learning what we each have spent our sixty plus years learning. Why not stand on our shoulders and simply apply what we have learned where it fits for you and go on from there?

The path of *freedom through relationship* is not for the faint-at-heart; in fact as you will read, it takes an enormous amount of courage. But it is doable and there are great benefits: deeper love and intimacy, more happiness, a freedom to be yourself and an underlying peace, satisfaction and gratefulness. Each of these benefits is won by hard work and a commitment to stay the course.

It requires an ability to observe your own thoughts and feelings, a willingness to tell the truth of what you observe and are experiencing, and a fundamental understanding of the nature of upsets and the structure of the ego. And most of all, a commitment to being free from all the negative programming and the dysfunctional behaviors that programming generates. It is a commitment to being happy, but not necessarily comfortable.

If you are not familiar with many of these ideas and practices, I suggest first reading this book for inspiration, then studying my earlier book *Living Awake* for an in depth treatise of the more fundamental concepts we use in this book. Concepts like: observing yourself in action, the fundamental choice between being a victim or being responsible, how declarations generate our personalities as well as many aspects of our experience, and many more. Then you might review the agreements we list at the end of this book and you will be ready to start on your own journey.

One last warning before you begin the book. Reading the material of this book may trigger some of your own unhealed wounds. That can be positive, if you use the opportunity to observe and explore these upsets, or negative, if you are unwilling to be upset.

Before you judge my or Diane's behaviors, I would ask that you consider two things. First, both Diane and I have been committed to freeing ourselves from our dysfunctional conditioning for most of our adult lives and have pursued many experiences to that end. And second, the reward for the work we have done together is to share a joyous and satisfying life.

With this book, we are defining one way to accomplish what you have always dreamed was possible: to experience happiness and the joy of deep love in your life.

We wish you all the best,
Landon Carter

Chapter 1

Opening to Big Love

"I always knew I'd find you, though I never did know how..."

- Kate Wolf, *Give Yourself to Love*

Diane ⌒

As the New Year, 2009 began, I relished the days I had set aside, time for solitude, writing in my journal, meditating and reading, my personal "beginning of the year spiritual retreat."

In those quiet days sitting by a crackling fire, I renewed my intention to find a true partner. I knew it would take courage and strength, but at least from all my life experiences, I had a lot of both. And something had healed since my mother's death—I felt freer and happier than I could ever remember.

On January sixth, the feast of the epiphany, as I was writing a deep dialogue with my soul, my soul urged me to *use all my gifts and to not hold back*. (The feast of the epiphany, January sixth, is a religious holy day celebrated as the date when the three kings arrived to meet baby Jesus. The word now has come to have secular meanings such as: an illuminating discovery or a revealing scene or moment.)

Those words reminded me of what Landon Carter, my trainer for the *Six-Day Course* with *est*, had said: *"use everything you've got to make a difference in life."* Thirty years had passed, but I still remembered his words. I made a note in the margin to try to contact him and thank him. I'd also never forgotten how handsome and dynamic he was and how I'd labeled him at the time as my "ideal man." Where was he now, I wondered?

Later that day, I found him on the Internet, looking older but softer, even a bit vulnerable. I noticed that he lived in New Zealand. He'd written a book, so I ordered it. I sent him an email through his website and thanked him for the difference he had made in my life thirty years before.

He emailed me back and said that he was in South America doing some work, but would send me the book when he returned home. It felt good to have made that contact again. How amazing that we could communicate across the planet so fast and easily.

What I didn't know was that he had just had a powerful shamanic healing and it had centered on his finding a relationship. *"You will find a true partner soon, but first you have some work to do,"* the Shaman had said.

A week later, I had a psychic reading for the New Year from a *Cellular Empath* named Tantra Maat. She told me that "Big Love" was coming, to get ready for it and that she saw it happening by the fall.

Well that sounds good to me, I thought. *What have I got to lose here? I'm going to prepare for that and see what happens.*

I had about nine months, the time it took to birth a new life. I set the intention that I would birth my own new life in that time and would be ready for this "Big Love."

In one of the advanced seminars I'd done with *est* years before, we'd had the assignment to "clean up our lives." This meant to clean your house, your yard, your car, cupboards, closets, desk, and papers, even to balance your checkbook. Also, in the *Six-Day Course*, Landon had challenged us to be unreasonable. I'd used both of those assignments through the years and had some amazing results.

So I took on the project of preparing for love to come into my life, without reservation. I didn't just have a yard, I had an eight-acre farm, and I worked hard on that too. In addition, I let go of old clothes and purposefully made an empty space in my closet. After all, if I really believed this "Big Love" was coming, he'd have to have somewhere to hang his clothes!

I wrote in my journal about what I believed in, who I was looking for and what I had to offer. I worked again to let go of baggage from the past and to heal relationships that needed healing. I practiced expressing love and appreciation everywhere I could—with family, friends, even strangers. After all, love was love.

I watched my thinking and kept a positive outlook, no matter what. And that was no small feat. I'd listen to women complain about how there "were no good men out there" and I'd say to myself, *nope, not believing that. I just need one. And, he's supposed to be on his way!*

I knew that I was looking for someone who shared my deep values, who wanted to stay awake and experience the wonder of life, and who had made an effort to let go of his baggage. A partner on this journey called life.

Late in the summer, as I was cleaning out a bookshelf, I came across Landon Carter's book, *Living Awake*, which I'd received months before. I picked it up and looked through it again. It was a good book, but it just didn't reflect his dynamic personality. *It needs more stories. The few stories he shared in it were powerful,* I thought.

As I looked at his photo on the back of the book, I felt a kind of tug at my heart, the same feeling I'd had when I first looked at the photo on his website. He looked handsome, strong and authentic as he stared straight into the camera. But he also looked kind of...vulnerable? It was hard to put my finger on it, but I thought, *it looks like he has gone through some challenges since I last saw him, like maybe life has not been all that easy for him.*

But then I remembered my ideas about improving his book. So I sat right down and wrote him a bold email. I figured he could handle it—he'd been an *est* trainer after all. I told him that I had some ideas to help him to make his book stronger and more dynamic. I thought we'd be emailing back and forth across the planet. But I received an email right back—he was in San Francisco, just a few hours away. We started working to find a time to get together to discuss the book.

In January, the psychic had predicted I was going to find "Big Love" by the fall. It was now September. After Landon's and my emails and a few phone conversations about the book, I thought with a start, *what if it is him?*

I slept out on a bed on my deck under the stars all summer. The thought that Landon could be the "Big Love" was so startling,

I lay awake for hours that night, unable to sleep, looking up at the night sky. Yes, he was on the path of personal growth, but he'd been strong and intimidating as a trainer. *Being with him would be like going into the lion's den*, I thought, as I tossed and turned.

But then I heard an inner voice, almost a chuckle, which said: *"Yeah, but when you get into the lion's den, you'll find out that he's really just a big pussycat that wants to be petted!"* Now that was interesting! I finally slept.

As we talked on the phone to arrange to get together, I could feel an easy rapport. I told him about my farm and he asked, *"So are you alone there?"* I answered that I was.

I didn't know if he was available. I kept telling myself—*you're just getting together to talk about his book. Don't get ahead of yourself.* But I also knew that he was the kind of partner I had been looking for and that if he was single, I was interested.

Landon ⌒

At the time Diane was opening herself to a new relationship and first thought about me after thirty years, I was in Ecuador having just come out of the equatorial jungle and a profound experience with the Achuar tribe in their natural habitat. With the assistance of Iawasca, (a combination of several plants used by indigenous people of Ecuador to initiate a shamanic journey), I had experienced the sense of oneness I had longed to have, that sense of awake presence and connection without any particular attachment to my body or the identification of "I." So after many years of "searching," I was feeling pretty complete as an individual.

As part of the Pachamama Alliance trip (Pachamama means mother earth) with my dear friends Bill and Lynne Twist, I was now standing naked in front of a mountain (Quechua) shaman in Otovalo, who had accurately read my life by holding a candle I had rubbed all over my body. He said, *"You were sad coming to Ecuador and your energy has been up and down. You have had lots of relationships and you will find your true partner soon, but first you have some work to do."* He next rubbed an egg over my body and then broke it to get rid of the bad stuff, and was now imbibing alcohol and blowing fire all over my body. I felt open to the healing and thought, *well we shall see.*

When I returned to New Zealand where I was living, I got some coaching from a woman who had been on the Ecuador trip, and for thirty days I did a ritual every day to bring in this "new partner." So when I re-met another former *est* trainer in San Francisco, I thought she might be it, and I moved in with her the summer of 2009 to see if in fact she was my "true partner."

We both tried, but it was a bit like oil and water, and after a long summer, it was clear to both of us that we were friends, but not a couple. I was just in the last days of moving out when I first met Diane to talk about improving my book, *Living Awake.*

It was fall, 2009, and I felt discouraged and unsure of my ability to choose a partner, after all, I had just failed one more time. And I was very "gun shy" about commitment having "tried" it so many times to no avail. So while I felt fairly whole and complete as an individual, I was very incomplete and unfulfilled in the domain of male/female relationships

Diane ‿⁊

Landon did competitive rowing and was going to be at a race about an hour from my home, so I figured I'd drive down and meet him at a Starbucks for our meeting. We'd have an hour or so conversation about the book and that would be it. But then he said he'd like to come up to my place, he had a van that he could sleep in, and he would spend the night.

He would spend the night. Now this was something completely different. We would have hours together, possibly a whole day, at my newly transformed home and farm—not just an hour in a coffee place. *Okay.*

I had about a week left before our arranged meeting. I hired my friend who'd been helping me clean up and clear out all year and we did a marathon of more clearing and cleaning. I wanted to feel as up to date as possible in my life when Landon arrived.

I had to smile that I was doing what I'd learned from *est*, to prepare for a big opening, to prepare for his visit.

He arrived in the late afternoon, driving into my driveway as the sun was setting behind the tall oaks and pines toward the west. I happened to be outside when he pulled in.

"Hi, welcome," I stammered, distracted by how the sun reflected in his green eyes. *Oh my God, he's still gorgeous.*

When he got out of his car, I liked the way his tall, strong body felt as we hugged. He followed me up the stone steps and into my hand-made house.

"This is beautiful," he said, as he surveyed my deck with the giant oak tree reaching up toward the sky, right through the redwood boards. He followed me into the kitchen and hopped

up onto the counter, as if he'd been there a hundred times before. I poured us some fresh mint tea and we walked out onto the deck and sat facing the sunset. I could feel him take in the silence and stillness of the farm.

As we sat and chatted, I kept having to come back into the present moment, sitting on my deck with him, feeling like I'd always known him, contrasted with the ideal man I'd put on a pedestal, and been intimidated by, thirty years before.

We decided to go out and have dinner. I called my favorite restaurant, the New Moon Café, and pleaded with them to get a last minute reservation. New moons are about starting new things. Maybe that would be good luck.

During dinner, he told me that he'd just ended a relationship. I was so happy to hear that—I hadn't had the courage to ask him. We chatted and laughed. He was a great listener and I ended up telling him lots of things about myself and my life, more than I usually would have told anyone that quickly.

There were a few moments during dinner when I could feel us really connecting. Even though we were having fun and it felt so easy, I wasn't sure if he was interested in me. But I knew that I was interested in him. When we got home, we ate an apple crisp I'd made from my own fresh apples, in front of the crackling fire.

He was going to sleep in his van. *"You should sleep out on the deck,"* I said. I had an old wooden couch that pulled out into a bed. He was happy with that idea, so I got the bed set up with sheets and a down comforter.

As he crawled under the covers, I looked up at the stars twinkling through the oak trees and blurted out, *"I so envy you sleeping outside. I just moved my bed off the deck a few days ago, in case it rained."*

"Well, climb in," he said.

Did he just invite me to climb in beside him? I paused for a half second, took a breath, then crawled in next to him, looking up at the twinkling stars. We lay there like a couple of pre-teens, shy and not touching, but talking animatedly for a long time, about the universe, our lives, nature. Then I remembered that he'd had a long day.

"You must be tired, I'll let you get some sleep," I said, as I crawled out and walked toward the door into the house.

"Thanks for the pillow talk," he said. I paused, one foot inside the door and looked back.

"Yeah, my favorite thing," I said.

"My second favorite thing," he said, and I laughed out loud. Was he flirting? I headed inside, chuckling.

I took a long hot bath, taking deep breaths, trying to relax. *Landon Carter, the Landon Carter, my ideal man for thirty years, is sleeping on my deck. Is that possible? Wow.* I crawled into bed and managed to get to sleep, then woke up at midnight with a start. I'd been having an intense, intimate dream and he was in it; it felt like he was there with me in my room. But as I lay there staring at the painted wood planks of the ceiling, feeling my heart beating fast, I realized, *no it was just a dream.* But he *was* outside on my deck. That was real. I was wide-awake.

From midnight till two in the morning, many different thoughts floated through my mind. But I came to an important resolution. He was leaving the next day after we talked about the book. I had to be bold and let him know that I was interested in him. Otherwise, he would leave and I might never see him again. He was headed across the planet to New Zealand in just over a week. I couldn't let this chance pass by.

I prayed to Saint Michael and asked for help in what to do. I was raised that girls didn't ever make the first move, but several times in my life I had and it had turned out well. That gave me courage. I slept.

I hopped up at six and made two cups of green tea and, still wearing flannel pajama bottoms and a t-shirt, took the steaming mugs out to the deck.

"I brought you some tea," I said.

"That sounds great," he said, and sat up on his elbow. I sat on the corner of the old bed. We listened to the quiet together and sipped our tea.

"Climb in," he said again. I crawled in beside him and took a breath. *Here goes,* I thought.

"Are you open to snuggling?" I asked. That seemed innocent enough. And if it just ended in that, what harm would be done?

"Sure, I'm open to snuggling," he said, so I moved up close to him and put my head on his chest. I noticed how well we fit together and I even liked how he smelled. I'd read somewhere you should like the way your partner smells. His strong arms felt so good around me as his chest pillowed my head. *This feels so natural,* I thought.

We snuggled and talked as birds chased each other across the sky, high above the oak trees, sunlight glinting off their wings. When the light hit the tops of the trees and lit up the leaves, we were still talking, comfortable and happy, lying there together watching the day begin. By the time the sunlight had moved down the trees and the squirrels scampered across the branches, busy hiding acorns, he gave me a soft, tentative kiss.

Oh goody, I thought, and gently kissed him back.

Chapter 2

The Beginning of a Love Story?

"Trust that you are being minded..."

-Diane's inner guidance

Diane ⌒

His kiss was tentative. I was open. We were adults—hey, we were both grandparents, alone on the deck with the trees, the birds and the sky.

By the time he left later that day, we'd discussed his book in detail, enjoyed the delicious fresh eggs from my hens, and shared some very precious, intimate moments looking into each other's eyes.

He had one weekend left before flying to New Zealand in eight days, and I invited him to come back and spend it with me. But he said no, he had too much to do, including something with the woman with whom he was just completing a relationship.

We'd just shared a magical time together and he wasn't moving heaven and earth to come back? Surely that must be a reflection on me, my mind screamed.

"Okay, if I never see you again, I want to have a way to hold this where I don't go into 'I'm not good enough,' because that's where my mind wants to go right now," I said.

We were lying on the couch outside on the deck. He was listening, with a towel over his head, to protect against the sun. I thought it also might be to hide a bit from me. He seemed confused and torn, not overjoyed at our newfound intimacy.

"So I'm going to think of what was great about our time together, to fight that 'I'm not good enough' default setting."

"We really had fun at dinner last night and there were moments when we connected." A grunt of agreement from under the towel.

"You're so easy and fun to talk to. It feels very natural being with you and having you here." He agreed again.

"I thought the book conversation went well." That was a yes too. *"And I feel a real connection with you."* He may have let that one go.

"There, that feels better now. If I never see you again, I can have those things to keep."

He took the towel off and looked at me. It seemed that my little conversation with myself had given him some freedom too. He moved a little closer.

I went on. *"And someone told me something that I thought was wise and true, about relationships: 'If you are meant to be together, nothing can keep you apart. And if you're meant to be apart, nothing can keep you together.' So there's nothing to worry about. We can relax."*

He smiled and put his arm around me. We went inside. As we made love for the second time that day, he looked into my eyes the whole time. No man had ever done that with me before and I felt mesmerized. I knew I might never see him again, but I knew I loved him and let myself feel that. *I love you, Landon Carter,* I expressed back to him through my eyes.

Later, as he got into his car, I invited him again to come back the next weekend, telling him we could go to the river and how beautiful that was.

"No, I can't. Too much to do before I leave."

"Okay then. Goodbye." I gave him a hug and a kiss. I watched his van disappear down the driveway. No matter what happened in the future, I felt excited and new from the time we'd shared.

Thank you universe. If he isn't the 'Big Love,' then could you please send someone just like him? Later that day, he sent me an email thanking me for the *"romantic, magical, fun, relaxing, nurturing time we had together."*

I wrote him back. *"I will always cherish looking into your eyes."* That was true. I would.

Then I waited. I was hearing a very certain, clear voice telling me exactly what to do, and what not to do.

"Give him lots of space," it commanded. *"Don't push him or crowd him,"* it went on.

Okay, I thought, interested that I didn't seem to be in this alone. And trusting that advice because it went against the reaching, grasping, neediness of my mind, which was whining somewhere in the background.

I'd learned about the power of intention from *est*. He said he couldn't come back, but I was holding the intention that he would. I bought almond milk, which he liked. I planned a delicious salmon dinner for Saturday night. I made sure I had candles, massage oil, wine. I bought him a book as a gift. On a whim, I bought a lacy thing I saw on a rack outside a lingerie store in town and buried it in a drawer—we'd see about *that*.

By Wednesday afternoon, still no word from him. On my end, my internal conversation alternated between the mind screaming and the calm certain voice, like two radio stations broadcasting in my head.

The strong clear voice said: *"Trust that you are being minded. If it is meant to be, he'll come. If not, you need to let go."*

Wednesday night, he emailed that he couldn't come. I cried, just for a few minutes and then let go, remembering what the voice had told me and also what I'd told him about relationships. *"If you are meant to be together, nothing can keep you apart. And if you're meant to be apart, nothing can keep you together."* I had to trust that I was being minded.

All the next day, Thursday, I kept holding the intention that somehow he would come. I was just getting ready to go to bed when the phone rang at ten o'clock. I could see from the caller ID that it was him.

"How would you feel about having a guest for the weekend?" he asked.

"Sounds great to me," I said, trying to sound nonchalant. *"We can go to the river. It will be fun."*

I hung up the phone and jumped around my living room. *Yipee! Hurrah! Yahoo!* Even though it was ten o'clock, I called a girlfriend and told her, *"He's coming! He's really coming!"* We whooped and hollered.

Friday, I scurried and cleaned and cleared again, getting everything ready. He'd be here on Halloween night, and a full moon. My teacher John O'Donohue taught me that on All Hallow's

Eve (Halloween) and the next day, All Soul's Day, the veil between the worlds is said to be the thinnest; it is a time when the power of magic is available and strong.

How great is that? I thought.

Landon ↝

When I first met Diane, there was certainly no rush of feeling, no "this is the one," but on the other hand, it wasn't a definite "no" either. It was a pleasant, friendly interaction with someone who was intelligent and "just on the scale of acceptable." Like most men, I had my scale of who was acceptable!

In the past, I had mostly seen my future partner across the room, felt attracted to her (some degree of those "falling in love" feelings), and pursued her. With Diane, there were no such feelings, but I did feel unusually comfortable and relaxed with her, I liked her farm, and it was easy to be myself.

During the times I was single, I was always "on the hunt," checking out each potential woman I met. And I was attracted to women who fit my pictures—athletic, blonde, skinny and about twenty years younger. Diane was six years younger than me and attractive, but just made the "acceptable" category, so it was not what I would have called a "strong start" by any means!

That we ended up snuggling, kissing and making love that first weekend was a bit rushed, but I figured "what the heck, we are both adults" and it was a good experience for us both. Perhaps, I was just demonstrating the typical male modus operandi of "any port in a storm," but the reality of my nurturing experience with Diane and her open, straight forward approach to life, in contrast to whether she fit my pictures, was ultimately what brought me back for more.

I drove down the driveway after that first weekend with my mind and emotions in turmoil. When we had made love, the connection felt strong and passionate and in those moments, Diane looked young and beautiful to me. But at other times, she didn't. The feelings of love were definitely there, as they had been with other partners.

But given my uncertainty from all the past failures, I couldn't authentically sustain that level of connection or commit to anything in the future. I just wanted to retreat, to re-gather myself, to not get in too deep, and to not give Diane false hope. So Diane's request for me to come back the next weekend was just too much, too soon. I couldn't wait to get away.

At that time, I was ending my previous relationship and was entertaining the fantasy of a relationship with a divorced woman who had teenage children. She fit my pictures, was twenty years younger and attractive, blond and thin, but after several phone calls and emails and a tentative lunch, we hadn't even kissed. I had also never been to her home nor met her children.

On the other hand, my experience with Diane was real. So I was caught on the horns of a dilemma between my tangible experience of Diane and the excitement of the "chase" after my pictures with all the accompanying feelings of desire, wanting, and uncertainty.

I had originally said that I could not come back for the second weekend with Diane before leaving for New Zealand, as I had planned to spend the time completing with my previous relationship. However, on that Wednesday night she and I had a great dinner and evening at the opera in San Francisco and I declared that as our completion—end on a good note! So suddenly, I felt free to explore the next steps with Diane.

Diane ⌣⌐

Landon arrived on Saturday afternoon and we drove down to the river. It was deserted, just the rocks, the sparkling fresh water, the trees, the sky and us. We jumped into the icy cold water, then lay out on warm granite rocks in the sun, enjoying the peace and beauty till the sun slanted low.

At home, we worked on the salmon dinner together in the kitchen, laughing and chatting. He built a blazing fire in the fireplace and we ate by candlelight, with the fire flickering in the background.

Like the first time, there was so much to talk about and I never had to stop and think of what to say. In the hours of the night of Halloween, we soaked in a large tub outside under the full moon, did a ritual with sage and frankincense and then gave each other massages in front of the fire. At the end of the evening, we made love, looking into each other's eyes in the firelight.

As we crawled under the covers outside on the deck and slept, I said a prayer to the moon that we would fit as easily into each other's lives as we fit into each other's arms.

The next day, we went back to the river, dipping into the icy waters, then basking again in the warm sun.

"This has been my whole summer in two days: the sun, the river, and you," he said.

But as much as he seemed to enjoy our time together, I could still feel his hesitation and reservation.

"Don't worry about that," the voice said. *"Just stay present with him, right here, right now."*

Good advice, that I did my best to follow.

He left late in the day to drive back to San Francisco and catch his flight to New Zealand the next day.

Our time together had been as magical as I could have imagined. And yet, as he left, I felt no certainty about what the future would hold with him. As my mind screamed, the deeper voice calmed me down.

Landon ⌒

I returned for the second weekend and that added another real and enjoyable experience to my slowly growing memory bank of who Diane was. We were becoming friends and lovers, but it was a long way from any sense that "Diane was it." I also really liked Diane's little apple farm and it turned out there was even a lake nearby where I could row! So the positive checklist was starting to fill in!

But again, by Sunday afternoon, I couldn't wait to get away. Yes, we'd had an amazing, magical and intense time together, at the river, out under the full moon and making love by the fire. But she seemed to want so much more than I did and I was afraid that she was making what we'd shared mean that we were somehow committed.

As good as it was, the sense of being in over my head and out of control frightened me, so I left that weekend with mixed feelings and inner turmoil. As I drove down the driveway, a sense of relief swept over me as once again I was on my own and I knew how to do "on my own."

Chapter 3

Sharing Magic

"You had me at hello."

- From the movie, *Jerry Maguire*

Diane ⌐

After Landon left for New Zealand, I didn't hear from him for days, then received a warm but vague email—a reference to good memories and maybe we could do it again sometime. . .

My mind screamed out in pain. *That's all he has to say?* it fumed. But the other clear, strong voice reassured me, *"No matter what it looks like, no matter what he says or does or doesn't do, Do Not Be Afraid. Keep holding the space open for him to come back and nestle into, a love nest of heart, soul, Eros and magic."*

That reminded me how John O'Donohue, in *Anam Cara,* said that the phrase *"do not be afraid"* recurred 366 times in the Bible. Because I'd lived so much of my life in a state of fear, the idea of living without it felt like a revelation.

As the month of November unfolded, Landon and I emailed sporadically back and forth across the planet and once in a while talked on the phone. Clearly, he wasn't as interested as I was in staying connected. I wrote a lot in my journal, prayed, and the wise, clear voice calmed me down.

"*It doesn't matter what it looks like now. It only matters how it turns out.*" That gave me the sense that it *could* turn out.

I wrote a letter to him in my journal:

I know how to do "alone." I know how to be involved with a man I can leave.

What I want to explore is true partnership, deep, intimate, soul burning love and tenderness, laughter, pleasure and bliss.

Could we have that together? We did have that together, so the answer is yes. Could we sustain that together? Why not? What are we saving ourselves for?

The good thing about being older and wiser is that we know we don't have time to waste. We know that love is precious, deep connections rare, and that rich physical intimacy is something to be treasured.

I don't want to tell you that I feel afraid sometimes, that I opened my heart, soul and mind to you and then you left. (How classic for me, who has a fear of abandonment.)

I don't want to tell you (but you must already know) that I feel tender with you, soft and juicy, willing to risk my heart, unafraid and fearless in spite of the quaking in my legs and belly.

I don't want to tell you that I could hold you in my arms and feel the bliss of that, over and over again.

I don't want to tell you that making love to you carries me away somewhere I recognize and have missed being for far too long.

I don't want to be the only one loving like this, and I wasn't when we were together that brief time, a taste of what was and could be.

But since you left, I feel the huge distance between us, words on a screen, your voice over the line and the question of how to say what I don't want to say in case I'm foolish.

But I'm not foolish. This is what I want, this energy, this Eros, this alive and awake meeting of life head on, fearless and afraid at the same time, quaking on the brink.

This is what I want. What do you want?

I could see and feel the future that we could have together. But could he?

A few days later, he mentioned in a phone conversation that he was planning to come back to the states without seeing me. In the pain of that hurt, I reacted and couldn't hide it. In the hour-long conversation that followed, he admitted that he was "gun shy" and that I was "one of his potentials." I listened and tried to understand as best as I could.

But he was acting out my very worst nightmare. I knew from all the workshops and therapy I'd done that the wounds from my childhood and my relationship with my mother were to feel invisible, unappreciated, and not good enough. He was hitting all three at once in a giant bull's eye.

As I wrote and tried to sort out all my feelings in my journal, by some grace, the calm voice kept me going. I was listening to something deeper and more real than the ranting of my mind. It reminded me of being kind to my mother, at the end of her life, no matter what she did. That training was helping me deal with him.

I sent him back an email that I hoped would calm him down and at least give us a chance of going forward.

"Maybe we're supposed to just share some magic for a while. I'm open to it as long as it is magical for both of us."

It was true. It was as if I could hear beyond our minds to where we connected deeply. So I hung on, even when he seemed barely in.

After that, our conversations were more relaxed and we made plans for him to visit over New Years. He would be staying ten days. One of my close friends was aghast. *"Ten days! You barely know him!"*

But I *did* know him, in a way that stunned even me. The same intuition that told me to contact him initially and told me to not give up was fine with him staying ten days. And my heart was already in way over my head. I remembered what the heroine said in the movie Jerry Maguire, *"You had me at hello."* He did. He had me at hello.

I kept writing, meditating, listening to the voice and writing down what it said. Sometimes the message made me uncomfortable, but it was always wise.

Voice—*"don't crowd him. Do your work and create more space for him to fall into."*

So I did a sacred "space clearing" that I read about in a Feng Shui book, to clear out the energy in my house. As I started the sacred ceremony, I asked the land and trees to bless me, this ceremony and us. *This or something better, but I want it to be him.* And I heard *"we do too."* That felt like a good sign.

My therapist, when he heard about my ten-day date said, *"What if he's just using you for sex?"* I could see how it could look like that. But it didn't *feel* like that. It felt *right*. And I trusted that. I'd listened to the voice of my mind for so long and where had it gotten me? Years alone. This was new. I had just turned sixty-one. I was going for new.

I was feeling a sense of aliveness and energy that I could own and did not have to lose. If it didn't work out with him, I'd just be that much more open for a real partner. But I prayed it would be him.

I decided that I would risk opening up to him without reservation, body, mind and spirit, when he came back. My mind was not thrilled with this decision, but *I* was.

Landon ⌒

Back in New Zealand, I felt hesitant to invest time and energy in a relationship where, from time to time, I had the experience "she isn't it." I was also put off that Diane seemed to want more validation of our connection than I was giving her, which in my mind meant she was "needy." The fact that she suggested we just "enjoy the magic while it lasted" helped put my mind at ease.

I enjoyed the reality of our interaction and felt open to seeing what happened, but I wasn't drawn to Diane the way I had been with other women. It was more a neutral feeling interspersed with times of wonderful connection, especially when we were making love. But that was not enough for me, as I was committed to making sure that I was completely satisfied at all levels if I was going to commit to "this being it." And for the two months apart, we didn't have that intense physical connection.

One of my frameworks for assessing whether we were a fit or not was the eastern system of the seven chakras. Did we connect at each chakra? One, security and trust; two, sex and pleasure; three, emotional empathy; four, our heart connection; five, deep, authentic communication; six, a shared vision; and seven, a spiritual connection at the level of Being to Being.

I had not really experienced what those connections would actually look or feel like for me to say, "this is it," but at least I had a system of sorts. In addition, I was committed to telling the truth as I experienced it and letting the chips fall where they may, for in the end, it was my life and I was committed to being authentic in it. I wasn't getting any younger, and when all was said and done, I was the one responsible for my own satisfaction.

But I had never had a partner who was up to dealing with things at the level that I was ultimately interested in. In fairness, I don't think in the past I was up to it either. I still felt too frightened and insecure to say what was really on my mind, even though in other relationships I had talked about many of these same concepts and tried to practice authentic communication.

Chapter 4

The Bumpy Road of Love

"Give yourself to love, if love is what you're after..."

- Kate Wolf, *Give Yourself to Love*

Diane ⌒

L andon came back, late on the 30th of December, after skiing with his son and friends, all lean and lanky, bundled up in a ski hat and parka. I welcomed him by a crackling fire. For Christmas, I gave him a granite, heart shaped stone, the color of his eyes and a wool hat I had knitted for him.

He gave me a jade Maori necklace from New Zealand, shaped in a spiraling, circular design that meant eternity and connection. He'd given the same necklace to his ex-wife and another female friend, so the significance of the gift didn't mean that much to him. But I loved it, put it on and wore it next to my heart. I would wear it continuously in the months to come as we journeyed together on the bumpy road of love.

New Year's Eve, we went out to dinner early and came back to make love and sleep in front of the fire. As we drifted off to sleep, I smiled as I remembered what Tantra, the psychic had said about Big Love by the fall and what I'd written as a goal— that I'd be in my partner's arms on New Year's Eve.

He'd told me how much he loved a traditional holiday dinner, so I'd bought a turkey and all the trimmings and the next day we prepared it together, inviting a couple over to share the feast, with a pumpkin pie fresh from a garden pumpkin.

For the ten days that we had together, we were mostly alone. He seemed to be as happy and comfortable to be with me as I was to have him there. We ate dinner by candlelight, laughing and talking.

They say that when you go deep with a partner, it drives up the layers of pain and wounds that are, as yet, unhealed. We were deep and close.

As we snuggled together in front of the fire after making love, he said, *"I'm going to the Bay Area next weekend to have lunch with a woman I'm interested in having a relationship with."*

"What did you say?" I sat up, stunned, watching the shadows of the firelight play on his face below me. He told me again.

"Do you have any idea how that feels to me? Just put a knife through my heart, why don't you?" I couldn't hold back the tears.

"No, I needed to tell you. We agreed to be totally honest with each other."

"Yeah, but you could have told me before you arrived, before I opened up to you like this and was so vulnerable."

"That may be true and I'm sorry about that."

I sat and breathed, trying to regain some composure, but wanted to scream.

Then I heard the voice again. *"Just get it,"* it said. It snapped me out of my own pain. *"Just get what he is saying."* Ironically, the concept of just "getting" someone's communication was something that I'd first learned in *est* years ago—that if you really heard what another person said, listened to their feelings without resistance or judgment, their feelings could get complete and could disappear. I'd experienced it happening over and over and felt very motivated for *these* feelings to disappear.

"*Okay,*" I said, taking deep breaths, trying to put a little distance between myself and the pain.

He told me how there was a woman he'd met the previous winter named Susan, who lived in the Bay Area with three teenage kids. He felt like he'd missed out on his own kid's teenage years because of his divorce. He and Susan had emailed and talked a few times and had agreed to have lunch to talk about the possibility of having a relationship.

Okay. It was the *possibility* of a relationship. As he talked about it, it became clear that they'd never had a date, kissed, or spent any time together. How much of a threat could that really be?

So I let it go. The new stronger me let it go, stunning my mind even as I did it. We were together, intimate by the fire. She was an idea in his head. *We'll see about that,* I thought. I lay back down and snuggled close to him.

Landon ⌒

As Diane and I became more intimate with candle light dinners, making love and sleeping in front of the fire, I started to feel the pressure of not being totally authentic and honest with her. In past relationships I had always been serially monogamous, ending one before starting another. I even considered that entertaining a fantasy about a next relationship, before completing the last one, to be somewhat out of integrity.

The fantasy of a possible relationship with Susan, which I'd held onto for almost a year, began to haunt me. I realized that I'd better find out if there was any reality with her before I got in any deeper with Diane. Given the intimacy we were sharing, I was feeling increasingly inauthentic.

I knew I needed to confront this very uncomfortable issue so that I could be one hundred percent, one way or the other. This was one of those conversations I knew would cause an upset and lots of hurt feelings, so I tried to plan it for a moment when we were feeling really good about each other and Diane would feel strong in our relationship. I certainly didn't want to lose the possibility of being with Diane in the future over what could end up being just a fantasy about Susan.

I'm sure that telling her after we had just made love, sounds like exactly the wrong time to say "I'm thinking about seeing someone else," but that is what I did in the name of being honest and authentic. Diane, being the champ she is, took it remarkably well and having said it, I was able once again to relax into the reality of our warm and nurturing experience together.

Diane ⌒

As a travel writer, I had an assignment to write about a nearby ski resort and hotel in Lake Tahoe. Because of the article, the resort gave us a lovely suite for two nights and three days, ski rentals, lift passes and dinners. We headed up the hill for the one-hour drive.

But after a day of skiing, he acted grumpy and withdrawn. We went back to the hotel and down to the hot tubs and he continued to ignore me, not talking or even looking at me.

"Look, if I'd wanted to be alone, I could have come by myself. It's no fun being with you," I said. It was the same at dinner— he was glum and wouldn't talk. I felt trapped. Back in our suite, sitting by the fire, I'd had enough.

"We need to talk. You're acting like an arrogant jerk. We're here in this lovely place together. It could be so romantic. What is going on with you?"

"If you were just Susan, then this would be perfect," he said.

That was it. I was furious. I so hated being seen as "the one he didn't want to be with." If I'd had a way to walk out on him right then, or to kick him out, I would have.

But we'd driven in his car and were an hour from home, over icy roads. I had no way to escape. If he left, I was stranded. And what was I to do? Walk out into the winter night alone? So I sat and breathed fire for a few moments, trying to calm down. I heard "the voice" pipe in while I was fuming:

"Isn't it interesting that this intense pain came up now, when you have no way to get away? You have to stay here and face it. Just notice that." I noticed it all right and didn't like it one bit. But the noticing did give me a tiny bit of distance from the pain. We sat next to each other in silence as my heart beat hard in my chest and I tried to find a drop of calm.

"Look, she's just a fantasy, some picture you have in your mind. You haven't even been on a date with her, kissed her, made love to her. You're sixty-six years old. Are you going to go to your grave with your 'pictures' or are you going to get real. I'm real, sitting here next to you, and what we have together is real."

"And another thing. I will go toe to toe with you and stand up to you. And you need that, when you are being a jerk, like right now. Can she do that?"

He looked at me—he knew I was right. He *was* being a jerk but just couldn't seem to help it. He seemed to snap out of it a bit and as we sat next to each other, my words hung in the space between us. It felt good to have stood up to him. I knew that what I said was true.

Then the new me kicked in and shocked my mind again, which still fumed. I moved closer to him. *"We're here together now. Let's not waste this moment."*

Something shifted. We talked about the day and what had gone wrong. He admitted to being a jerk. We started again, back to the closeness we'd had before. That night, we slept tangled up together, all night.

The next day, driving back in the car, I said I needed to talk and he agreed.

"My coach says that true soul mates are not the people you're all lovey-dovey with, but the people who push you to do deep soul work. Maybe I can help you to untangle this thing you do where 'she isn't it.'" In this case, the *"she"* who wasn't *"it,"* was me, but still. . .

He was still planning to leave and to go and meet Susan on the weekend. So I added, *"And if you leave and end up being with her, you can't come back. That's it for me. I'm ready for a deep and powerful relationship with someone who loves and values me. And if it is not you, then I need to move on."*

It felt so good to set some boundaries and to stand up for myself again. We had a close couple of days before he left, where I kept letting go when my mind wanted to be upset about his leaving.

I heard the voice as I wrote in my journal.

"You have to trust completely. Whatever he does, does not reflect on you. It reflects on his process of discovering the truth for himself. Stay strong."

The morning he left, I kissed him goodbye and wished him well.

"If this is goodbye, it's been great. I have no regrets."

He thanked me for giving him the space to go and said that he felt accepted. I waved to him from the porch. I felt unattached.

If he didn't come back, it would be hard, but I would survive. I had great friends and a good therapist. As my teacher John O'Donohue had taught me, I knew I was being minded or looked after somehow. I had to trust in that.

Landon ⌒

When I left for the Bay Area to meet with Susan, I felt very conflicted about what I should do. Susan wasn't even answering my calls and the more I thought about it, the more it was apparent that I was holding onto a fantasy of what could be with her, in contrast to the reality of what I had with Diane. Susan and I were supposed to get together, but she was giving me no indication of interest on her part. What was I thinking?

That weekend, I never actually spoke with Susan or saw her while I stayed in the Bay Area with friends. And when I saw her several years later at a function, she hardly recognized me

—that's how shallow our connection was! Yet at the time all of this was occurring, she seemed to be a real possibility. Such was the strength of that fantasy, especially when it fed some ego identity that I wanted—the younger, blond, skinny wife, who fit my "pictures."

I was afraid of aging and though Diane is almost six years younger than I am, her wrinkles reminded me of my own aging. Also I had wanted the relationship with Susan's teenage children in some attempt to recapture what I had missed with my own children, a second try at doing it better this time.

In addition, as an aging, competitive athlete, I have found it difficult to find the balance between pushing my limits in my training as my abilities decline and aging gracefully. So I think I was drawn to the energy of a more youthful partner in an unrealistic effort to recapture my own youth.

Also there may be some deep-seated male programming about being the old bull male taking the young wife to procreate the tribe! Anyway the attraction was there on my part, even though many of these younger women may not have been interested in me, as I found out with Susan.

Diane ⌒

Landon left in the morning. That night, he called and left me a message.

"I'm thinking of you fondly," he said, his voice warm and loving. I loved that, but also felt a bit confused. What about this other woman?

Saturday he called again.

"I'm in. I love you and miss you and want to come back and talk about being together and having the best life possible. I can see now that the other was just a pipe dream and isn't going to happen. I miss you."

I felt happy, amazed and a bit stunned.

"I love you," he said, before he hung up.

"I love you too, you rascal," I said.

He came back two days later. In those first few moments, I felt some fear, then heard the calm voice again.

Voice—*"Can you handle just this moment?"*

Me—*"Yes of course."*

Voice—*"And the next moment?"*

Me—*"Of course."*

Voice—*"That's it then, moment by moment. That's the secret. That's all that you need to be able to do."*

Me—*"I can do that."*

I told him about that inner conversation and it seemed to break the ice a bit and take the pressure off. He must have been nervous too. We had a delicious reunion, both of us excited at the new opening and possibility. As the days unfolded together, it felt intimate, powerful and sweet.

We had one difficult bump when we were out at a dance and he went into his "she isn't it" again. I felt it when he did it, and lost confidence in myself, making it even harder. Then he withdrew. When we got home, I insisted we talk and sort it out.

He admitted that he was looking around at other women that he wanted to dance with and that he thought were more attractive than me. He said that he felt trapped and afraid that he'd lost his freedom. I just listened and tried to understand.

But I was also learning some boundaries and strengthening my ability to stand up for myself.

"When you go into those thoughts, I feel like I'm trapped into a net of your negative projection and it feels terrible—stifling and confining. Don't do that. I hate it."

We sorted things out and I let it go. We ended up close again. At least we were talking about it all and nothing was being swept under the carpet.

I liked the tender, softer place that had opened up in me. I'd never felt that with a man before and it was also the opposite of how my mother had treated my father.

I wrote in my journal: *"I'm standing on the brink of a new life, with a man I love. I can see the stepping stones and the thread is love and tenderness and having a heart that is healed enough to open again, in spite of the risks."*

Landon ⌒

Just because I had the experience of loving Diane and really liking who she was and what we shared together, and even declaring, "I love you," did not mean that my ego was going to give up and say, "OK, you have gotten what you always wanted, I can stop looking and searching now."

As I had written in my book, *Living Awake,* I was addicted to the hunt and the chase after some illusive future, addicted to the experience of being dissatisfied and looking for satisfaction. And as I would later uncover, I was deeply attached to the decision I made at birth that "this isn't it." But at the time, I did not understand my programming at that depth, so I would keep bringing up evidence to confirm the dismal conclusion—that Diane "wasn't it."

Now that the fantasy of Susan had been pierced through, I was still plagued by my wandering mind's looking for the next beautiful woman to attach itself to. This of course meant Diane wasn't the one and I was trapped in the situation of being with her, said my mind. So I felt dissatisfied and would close down.

Our agreement to tell the truth and be transparent, as uncomfortable and potentially relationship ruining as it seemed to be was, never the less, the path to freedom. But while we were in the middle of it, it felt at times like a form of hell!

.

Chapter 5

Across the Planet and Down

*"And the day came when the **risk** to remain tight in a bud
was more painful than the **risk** it took to blossom..."*

- Anais Nin

Diane

The last two days before he left to fly across the planet again, we were deep and close. I gave him two CD's of love songs that I had put together on my iPod and that we'd listened to. I hoped they would remind him of our intimate time together.

Then I loved being alone again, to digest and savor how much had opened up with his visit. We'd talked about the possibility of me going to visit him in New Zealand—he'd be gone six weeks, but I wasn't sure.

When days passed and I didn't hear from him, my mind wanted to flee into drama, but the calm voice kept telling me to *"trust, let go, relax and lighten up."* I chose to stay with it—so much wiser and much more fun than my screaming mind.

On the third day with no word, I sent him a brief *"How was the trip? How are you?"* His response was that he was busy and would call when he got his head above water. Two sentences, brief and rather cold. I freaked out but tried to be strong.

After another day and a half, I asked him if he was also withdrawing and not just busy and could we please talk about it if he was withdrawing? Then he sent me an email from his ex-girlfriend Julie's house, the one he'd told me he had really good sex with when they had been together, and I got scared and insecure. Ouch. So hard to see my own stuff coming up so fast and hard. I was certainly proving the theory that when you get in deep, the deepest wounds come up.

While we hadn't discussed the issue of being monogamous, I sensed that he would not be with another woman while we were exploring our relationship. It wasn't an issue for me—I was not interested in other men. I also knew that he would at least tell me the truth about it. It turned out that he was at his ex-girlfriend's house to use her Internet connection and to see her son. He was also still good friends with her.

The voice calmed me down. *"It's okay, you're human. Your mind is terrified of how open and vulnerable you are and is looking for any excuse to close down and run away. But you can be stronger than that."*

Lots of writing and staying deep and quiet helped. I wrote: *What if this is about staying in my heart and tenderness, no matter what?*

Six days passed and I suffered a lot from the lack of connection. The thing that kept me going with him was that when I was fed up and expressed myself authentically, he listened and could even shift. I did that on our next phone call.

"You know absolutely nothing about women, are wasting this relationship and I'm ready to give up," I said.

He admitted that he'd been "reluctantly backing in" to the relationship, but that what kept him taking the next step was the real interactions we had, especially when difficult things came up.

Lots got sorted out in that phone conversation and we were on better ground. I was encouraged enough to consider going to visit him in New Zealand. That would involve traveling for almost twenty-four hours and an expensive airline ticket. But I was willing to risk. And the calm, clear voice kept encouraging me.

"Be the space of the Divine Feminine that you came here to be, that loving, juicy, alive, very powerful and perceptive space."

And when I told the truth, even with the pain, the challenges, and the roller coaster, it felt like I was burning off old karma around relationships, and feeling my power in new dimensions. As I stood up to him, I felt my strength. As I stayed open to him, I felt myself softening, becoming more tender. The intensity and even the paradoxes fascinated me and compelled me to stay in.

After the conversation where I'd told him he knew nothing about women, he went from resisting talking to calling me every night. Stunned by the shift, I asked him about it.

"I'm enjoying it. I have surrendered to loving you. I'm impressed with your partnership."

After that conversation, I had to go to see him. The next night, saying goodbye, he said: *"All right darling, I love you."*

Was this the same man that a week before didn't want to talk, didn't want to email? Was he schizophrenic? Was I crazy to love him? I had to trust again, that it didn't feel crazy, it felt right. I booked my flight to New Zealand.

When I looked deeply at my own reactions, it felt like I was unraveling my mother's pain of "not being good enough" to heal myself. That all the family pain I'd carried for so long was coming up to be released.

It felt wonderful to discover my strength, in real life, not in theory. And in the strongest test of all, in love. But this journey I was on with him was not for the faint of heart.

I counted the hours, excited and dreamy about being in his arms again. I was going from winter to summer, flying over the International Date Line, leaving on February 13th and arriving on the 15th, skipping Valentine's Day. That could have been an omen, but in our new, connected space, I couldn't imagine that then.

Landon ⌒

One of my patterns had been to seek connection, usually through sex, and once satisfied and again validated that I was OK, withdraw. When I went back to New Zealand, this pattern emerged and was easy to justify by all the things I had to do there, having been away.

But as the days passed and Diane and I continued to have powerful talks, I became comfortable with our "at a distance" level of connection. As I was sitting in meditation one day, I had the insight that I needed to surrender to love. I'd listened to a song sung by Andrea Bocelli that inspired me and brought tears to my eyes every time I heard it, *"Go where love goes, go where your heart leads, Angels are begging you to go there."* So I told Diane, "I am surrendering to loving you" which prompted her to make her reservations to come to New Zealand.

Diane ⌒

When I landed and got off the plane, I threw my arms around him but he barely hugged me back. He avoided eye contact as we waited for my bags to arrive and it felt stilted and awkward between us. By this time, after traveling for over twenty-four hours, I was exhausted, but also wired and super sensitive.

We got into his van and as we drove, I'd reach out to touch him and he'd recoil, not returning the warmth at all. I finally asked him to pull over so that we could talk.

He told me that when I got off the plane and he saw me, he panicked. The whole conversation came up again in his head about how I didn't "fit his pictures" as he watched me walk towards him.

I couldn't believe what I was hearing. *I'd traveled across the planet after he'd said "I surrender to loving you," to be greeted with this?* At that moment, if I could have turned around and gotten back onto the plane to fly home, I would have. But by then, we were already miles from the tiny airport in Nelson where I'd landed, and I didn't have a ticket back. My mind wailed.

Landon is a pilot and I'd told him how much I'd always wanted to ride in an open-air biplane. So he'd bought me a ride with a friend whose business was to take people up in a two-seater open-air biplane. That sounded great. But then I found out that it was a ride to do stunts—rolling and twirling sideways and upside down in the open-air plane. In addition, though the pilot had a set of controls, I would be controlling the plane during the stunts!

By then I felt so angry with Landon that I was determined to do it, just to show him. I was terrified as I got into the flight suit, not even wanting to think about what I was about to do. It felt like the challenges of the *est Six-Day Course* all over again—jumping off mountains.

I went up in the small, open plane, admiring the views of farms, ocean and sky, teeth chattering and legs quivering about what was ahead. I screamed each time I pushed the control stick and we went over—it was videoed and I'm very loud, but I *did* it.

After the plane ride, we drove the rest of the way to his place, almost two hours, pretty much in silence. The lush green valleys and sunny beaches of New Zealand passed by outside the van, but I barely saw them. I was trying to sort through my jumbled emotions and come to a place of calm, but couldn't find calm anywhere. I just wanted to run and hide, like a wounded animal. And the exhaustion and jet lag didn't help.

Landon ∽

When Diane got off the plane and walked towards me, rather than the love, desire or yearning I thought I should feel, I felt a sense of panic. Once again, I thought, *Oh no, she isn't it and now what do I do?* I had gotten ahead of myself in what I had committed to when I'd told her I'd surrendered to loving her. I felt trapped in a situation I had created.

I'd had several relationships in the past in which early on I'd felt "she isn't it." In each one, I'd tried to overcome that feeling and was successful to a degree as I got to know and appreciate each woman, but in the end each relationship had ended with my forgone conclusion, "she isn't it." At that moment in the airport, I had that sinking feeling in my stomach, *here I go again down a path to failure.*

With all these feelings swirling around in me, I didn't want to give Diane false cues or lead her on, so I wouldn't hug her. My fear of commitment was surfacing big time, but I wasn't awake enough at the time to see it. I was only seeing the apparent evidence, my perception of Diane and my feelings, and unconsciously acting out the deeper fear.

I was afraid to tell Diane what I was feeling as it would hurt her feelings, get me in trouble, and create a huge upset, so I withdrew and closed down, hiding my "conclusion" from Diane. I felt trapped and depressed (suppressed anger at myself) for getting myself into this predicament and wouldn't even touch her. I am not a very good actor in terms of hiding my feelings and pretending all is well. I just withdraw further into my shell.

I had trained myself to be "nice" in past relationships when feelings were suppressed and issues unresolved, so I thought I could get by, show Diane an enjoyable time in New Zealand— after all it is a lovely country—and then send her home and be done with it. But Diane, bless her soul, would have none of it and on the way home made me pull the van over to the side of the road to talk.

This was one of those extremely uncomfortable situations where I would have rather not revealed the truth, as it only seemed to my mind that things would get worse. But once again, thanks to Diane's insistence, my telling her what was on my mind started the process that would eventually free us.

After talking beside the road in Motueka, I felt some reduction of the trapped feeling from being dishonest and inauthentic. While I knew Diane was still suffering from what I had said, at least things were out in the open to be dealt with and the slow process of healing was once again on a positive track. It would take us almost two days to finally come up with a solution that worked for us both.

Before getting home that first day and after all her hours of travel, Diane took me up on an offer to fly with a friend of mine in his aerobatic biplane. She did it just to spite me, I think and to show me that she was not going to let me get her down or be limited by her fears.

I was starting to learn how courageous she is in life, especially in the area of communication when the energy was off between us, as she would initiate an interaction where I would just withdraw and try to figure it out.

Once she asked, "What is going on?" I would reluctantly give a truthful answer. So I was at least up to telling the truth, which ultimately allowed things to clear up, as we would prove to ourselves over and over.

Diane ⌣⌐

Back at his house, he kept his distance. All my abandonment issues and wounds felt open and painful. I told him I felt set-up—that I flew across the planet to be with him after he'd said he'd surrendered to loving me—and then he changed his mind. When we went to bed that night, he wouldn't touch me and I lay there in agony. I told him that he felt like a huge bird with a very broken wing and that I wasn't sure I could help him to heal it.

I got up and wrote in my journal to try to sort things out for myself.

He's like a sea anemone, open, closed, open, closed. The only thing that has kept me here is the open. It's like being abused. Why do you stay? I asked myself. *Because when he's good, he's sooo good.*

I prayed to Saint Michael. The voice calmed me down. *"Just be his friend. Let him heal. Be generous, loving and kind. This is not forever for you either. So your mind can relax. Just do it moment by moment."*

All the next day he kept his distance. I looked out the window at the green hills of New Zealand, watched the sun sparkle on the ocean below and wrote in my journal. When I thought of our predicament—his fear and my pain, I had an image of two balls of yarn that had gotten all snarled up together. What if we could unravel it all, allowing us both to heal? Then we could see whether or not we wanted to create something healthy together.

By the end of the day, I had an idea and over a candlelight dinner, suggested it to him. I had nineteen days left of my trip. What if we held it as "the nineteen-day experiment"? We would tell the truth and try to unravel what was going on, moment by moment. I would be "in" one hundred percent for that time, but he had to agree to be "in" one hundred percent, too, beyond his fears, like we'd been in California together. Then, at the end of the trip, we'd see where we were.

He agreed, and I felt happy. Then he added his caveat. His answer was yes, as long as he had an "out," at the end—as long as there was no future commitment.

It wasn't perfect, but I was willing. After all, I might be the one who wanted the "out," based on the way he was acting. And I knew that I'd learn and grow and be that much more ready for a true partner, if it wasn't him.

So we agreed. I added to the agreement that we would have a passionate love affair and agree to always love each other, no matter what happened, even if we didn't end up together. He agreed to that. It is ironic that my experiences with *est* and the *Six-Day Course* are what gave me the foundation to take a risk like that and know that I could learn and grow from it, no matter how it turned out.

With our agreement in place, the space between us felt light and alive again. We talked openly all during dinner, flirting and laughing and then made love that night, regaining some of the closeness we had experienced in California. He thanked me for hanging in there and acknowledged me for being open to considering things about myself, which I am.

Landon ⌒

Somehow by agreeing to "the 19-day experiment" with no commitment at the end, my mind relaxed in a kind of truce over the question of, "is she it or not?" It calmed my fear that I was adding energy and agreement to a relationship that had some indications that it wasn't "it." I could put that decision on hold during her visit.

We could now go for it one hundred percent, let it all hang out in the truth telling department, and see what happened as a result. I had always believed in the adage that "the truth shall set you free," but had never found a partner with whom to dance that dance. Finally, I was with someone who was courageous enough to go that deep.

The further agreement that we would have a passionate love affair, always love each other and part friends were further benefits in an offer I could not refuse. I had planned on being with Diane for the nineteen days anyway and we were certainly going to learn something in the process.

Chapter 6

The Eye of the Needle, The Eye of the Storm

"The course of true love never did run smooth..."

-Shakespeare

Diane ⌒

Our passionate and intense lovemaking made the other times, when he still couldn't look at me because then he'd see how I didn't "fit his pictures," even more painful. I had struggled with low self-esteem my whole life and now had manifested a man who spoke those very fears loud and clear. *Oooh, ouch.*

It was true that my body wasn't perfect. It was also true that since I'd met him a few months before, I'd slimmed down—I'd been exercising and had lost fifteen pounds. But it still wasn't enough, it seemed. I'd never be that "young, skinny blonde" that he wanted in his pictures.

His body was beautiful for his age, slim, yet muscular and strong. But from all the athletics he'd done his whole life, he had ankle and knee pain which made him walk stiffly. I'd see that sometimes, but chose to focus on his good qualities. I so wished he could do that with me, but he couldn't.

In the face of his resistance, I had to find a sense of my own beauty. I was attractive, and if he couldn't see that because of his projections, then he was just plain missing out. That felt good. We didn't fight—we talked and listened to each other and that was pretty miraculous. If we could keep that up, who knew what could happen?

It was special to be there with him in his home, so far from mine. His place sat on a hill up above the ocean, quiet and peaceful, down a country road. We were alone there and I loved the intimacy, of making food together, cleaning up, sharing space, time, and experiences—even hanging my clothes in his closet. It made me see how ready I was to share my life with a man. On the good days, I hoped it would be him.

But our time together still felt like an emotional roller coaster. He would withdraw and get cold and I would have to face that and make him talk about it. Then he'd open up again and we'd be close. But it seemed that the closer we got, the more his pain would come up in the form of "I wasn't it" and he'd retreat again. On the challenging days, I'd be counting the days left of the "experiment." On the happy days, I didn't want it to end.

He had a theory that, through the "law of attraction," people attracted partners who allowed them to complete their deep issues. If his theory was true, then I'd attracted him in order to complete my own pain, my own insecurities about myself. I was willing to consider that. It reminded me of my days in *est* and in the training that he'd led, where I was confronted as a way to grow.

In spite of the challenges, I was feeling tender, soft and good. Our commitment to telling the truth to each other and to not hiding things created deep, intense conversations. Because

we weren't blaming each other, or at least
were, as long as we were able to keep talk...
some resolution.

But we still had different realities that needed sorting out.
When I wanted to connect, he called it "lovey-dovey" or "needy."
I called it simply "connecting." One day, I'd had enough.

"You know nothing about women," I told him again in
frustration. He had two brothers, had gone to an all male prep
school, to Yale when it was all men and to Harvard Business
School when it had two percent women—twenty-eight out of
fourteen hundred. *"Women like to connect and be related and
that is not needy!"* That led to a vibrant discussion where, in the
end, he admitted that I was probably right.

On the seventh day, when he ignored me and acted grumpy,
I was feeling very discouraged and that it was just too hard. If
I'd been closer to home, I would have left. But I was across the
planet, almost three hours from the closest airport.

As I wrote in my journal, the voice was right there, as always,
with words of encouragement:

Voice—*"You're really good for him. You wake him up and
shake him up. He hates it and loves it all at the same time."*

Me—*"I sense that if we do get through this, it could be easy."*

Voice—*"Yes, easy and good, very, very good."*

We drove into the mountains where he was teaching gliding
for a few days near St. Arnaud. During the three-hour drive, he
wouldn't talk to me. When I asked him about it, he snapped that
he was busy driving. I knew more was going on but couldn't get
him to open up, so stared out the window and struggled to hold
back the tears. How did I get myself into *this*?

After we settled into our hotel, he left for the day and I felt relieved to have a break from him. Our sunny hotel room had a lovely view of woods and a creek and I had a bike to ride and an alpine lake to swim in. I felt very content alone, like a cat, curled up in the sunny room, writing in my journal and getting myself centered and grounded.

During my writing, I did a dialogue with him, a technique that I'd learned in a journal workshop years before, a way to communicate with a person's higher self. It went like this:

Landon— *"Please don't give up on me. I couldn't stand another failure or to lose you."*

Me— *"You'd sure never know it."*

Landon— *"I know. I know it's hard. Please be patient. It's like I'm struggling to get out of a box."*

I took those words in and hoped they were true.

We were supposed to have a "date" that night, to be together and have some intimate time. I'd washed my hair and taken time to make sure that I looked my best. When he got back in the evening, he wouldn't look at me, made no acknowledgement that I looked pretty and didn't hug me or touch me. At dinner, he told the woman at the restaurant that *she* looked lovely, which made me feel even worse, even more invisible.

After an evening meeting with his gliding group, where we couldn't talk, we came back to our room and got into bed. I felt sad, anguished and angry and asked him what was going on. It was a blessing that I'd spent the day alone, getting strong and calm. I would need all my strength that night.

"I never wanted this relationship, I don't see us together, and don't see you as my partner. When we are walking down the street, there is no 'us,'" he said.

"But what about 'I am surrendering to loving you,'" I asked? *"If I'd known you felt this way, I would not have come to New Zealand."*

I lay there, stunned by his words. My mind cried out in pain, which made me start praying to Saint Michael—I couldn't think of what else to do. Between the pain and the praying, I was quiet.

As I prayed, I could feel the centered, grounded voice talking to me. *"Isn't this interesting how these really painful times always happen when you can't escape? Don't you find that mysterious? You're here, three hours from his home, with one car, just like when you were skiing in Tahoe and then again, when you got off the plane. Notice that."*

It *was* mysterious. Could it be that I was being tested only at times when there was no escape? Was this more evidence of being "minded" if I really looked closely? Was something larger than just my own little life going on here?

Meanwhile, my mind wailed at me to leave right that instant, to walk out the door and into the night. I followed that thought and pictured myself walking alone in the pitch-black darkness on the two-lane highway in the mountains of New Zealand. *No, can't do that.*

When that idea wouldn't fly, my mind started planning that as soon as we got back to his house, I should get to the airport and fly home, get away. No more of this pain. I deserved better... on and on.

I lay there fascinated with the two distinct stations in my head, one calm and clear, the other screaming and flailing. I was very familiar with my mind—I'd lived with that voice my whole life. Again, the new and different voice felt powerful and undisturbed.

At a deep level, I also knew that it was good that he had been able to say all that. That I just needed to listen, to get it all and not resist it, so I prayed to be able to do that.

In the silent gap between us, he asked how I was doing.

"I'm praying," I said.

"Is there anything I can do for you?" He must have known how hurtful his words were.

"If I think of anything, I'll let you know," I answered. I thought of asking him to hold me, but, at that moment, decided that wouldn't help.

As we lay next to each other, in silence, something in me softened towards him. That was not rational, under the circumstances, but I was tired of my screaming mind. I liked the other voice. I moved over and put my head on his chest, just for a moment, then said goodnight. I was not going to react to what he said. Not just yet.

Landon ⌒

The night in St. Arnaud was reminiscent of other times when relationships had ended. As soon as Diane started asking me about why I was cold and withdrawn, I felt under attack and hopeless about how to change myself to be warm and open so that she would not be upset.

I felt I was never going to meet her expectations of me and was hurt and angry about being "not good enough" one more time. So what I finally did say was some kind of ego defense that would allow me to maintain my deep patterns and stop being threatened by Diane's probing.

I felt sad, discouraged, and deeply disappointed that I had gotten to this state of relationship failure one more time. The things I had said to her—that she didn't fit my pictures and that I didn't want to be in a relationship with her—I couldn't take those back or explain them away. And I definitely couldn't see my way out of this dark place I had gotten myself into.

I felt totally closed down, almost as if I was mentally in a fetal position, hoping things would just end or clear up if I slept. In spite of the reservations I'd just expressed, a part of me didn't want the relationship to fail, and that gave me the incentive to try anything to make it work, even though I felt hopeless.

Everything was so fragile at that moment right after I told her "I never wanted this relationship" and "there is no us." I could feel Diane's pain, so without denying my experience or refuting what I had said, I asked, "Is there anything I can do for you?" It was my attempt to reach out, to say I was sorry for what she was going through, and perhaps repair a little of the connection that had been so dramatically broken. But I was at my wit's end as to what to do.

Somehow, by communicating what we were experiencing moment by moment and continuing to responsibly look at our own part of the upset, we got through it. I thank God for Diane's strength and persistence. Even though she was in pain and her mind was screaming at her to run away, she stayed calm and continued to look for the truth.

And she continued to stay open to me, which at the time was a miracle, since I certainly didn't deserve it, given the way I was acting. She called it "trying to unravel the tangled and snarled ball of yarn that had us bound up."

Diane ⌒

I dozed off and two hours later, woke up with a start. He woke up at the same instant. The sleep had given me some clear insights.

"All those things you said to me, about how I'm not it—those are just thoughts," I said. *"What we have between us is real and good."* He listened.

"And I'm an attractive woman and if you can't see it, then there's something going on there that is not the truth, that is just your own resistance."

We went back to sleep.

I woke up again at four and went downstairs to the living room to write and try to sort it all out for myself.

As I wrote, my mind cried out in pain, seething and angry. It had formed a plan: *Leave, as soon as you get back to his house. Get to the airport, onto a plane and don't look back. Then, as soon as you get home, get involved with someone else right away.* (It even came up with the names of two different men who were good options, men I'd flirted with in the past, before Landon and I had gotten involved.) *Either of those men would be better than he is, they won't treat you like this. And then, if he tries to win you back, you can slam the door in his face because you've already replaced him.*

Even though that scenario was tempting to my hurt and wounded ego, as I wrote down the words and felt their energy, I could sense how reactive they were. There would be no completion or resolution in that solution. The truth would not be so filled with anger and retaliation. So I knew that could not be the answer.

As I sat in the pre-dawn stillness and poured it all out into my journal, I could feel my newly discovered strength—how I could right myself after one of those painful experiences and keep looking for the truth.

What if this relationship was so powerful that both of us were really scared—his thoughts that I wasn't "it" and my wanting to run away? I saw too many mysterious coincidences that had made us not able to escape each other in the situations of our deepest pain.

I wrote, *we're at rock bottom deep issues here, real work that could be life altering if we're courageous enough to keep looking, putting our feet to the fire and telling the truth. Let's clear this stuff out, once and for all—that's the opportunity.*

During that quiet time alone, I could see that the new intimacy I'd found with myself was something I would never lose. And that I was able to be tender with him, and yet not let him get away with anything. I curled up on the couch to sleep, in case I needed to write some more.

He came down the stairs and asked me how I was. He'd been awake, waiting, the whole time that I'd been downstairs. So I went back up.

When we got back into bed, I told him, *"You may not think I'm "it" but I go toe to toe with you, hang in there and keep looking for the answers—how to unravel this and try to find the truth."*

He reached over and touched me and said, *"Thank you for going toe to toe with me and not giving up, otherwise I'd be abandoned in my own pain."* That moment felt tender, real and good.

"It would have been so much easier if you'd said, 'This is my pain, please just hear it and don't abandon me.' But you didn't say it that way and it caused me a lot of pain," I said. He listened and agreed.

"And the feeling of connection between us now, just that little touch and those true words, that is what I want. How ironic that it had to come after all this?"

We agreed to talk more in the morning and to try to get some sleep.

In the morning, he left to row, giving me more time to think and write. I fixed us some breakfast and was ready to talk when he came back. I said, *"let's agree to be "in" at least till we get home to your place."* I was still considering the option of bailing out of the rest of the nineteen-day experiment unless things really turned around. He said, *"at least till we get home,"* which surprised me. In other words, he was open to being "in" for longer.

As we talked about the night before, he said that he couldn't act how he didn't feel. I told him that I didn't want him to "act" and hated it when we were off and didn't just come out and talk about it.

"I'd rather not make love at all than to make love on top of stuff that doesn't allow us to connect. I'd rather have a gentle touch like you did earlier and a few tender words than make love without connection."

This is when we had a breakthrough.

He said, *"if you can really do that and let me be real so that I don't feel like I have to be something that I'm not, then that would be a first."* He told me that his pattern of "she isn't it" had caused all his relationships to break down right where we had been the previous night and he'd never gotten through it with anyone.

He'd had women hit him, scream at him, run away out into the night—all the behaviors that had run through *my* mind the night before. He thanked me for understanding him at a deeper level than any woman ever had. Otherwise, I'd just be the next victim on his pile of failed relationships that I didn't know was stacked up behind me.

I told him I would do my best to let him be himself, as long as we could talk honestly and openly about it all. If I needed to reach out to him, I would and if he didn't like it, he could tell me and we'd just try to stay present with each other and see what opened up.

"I never abandon you. Do you notice that?" I said. He seemed to notice.

Landon ⌒

After this horrendous night we had just gone through, I went off to row Lake Rotoiti which takes about an hour and a half to the end and back. I felt good after my exercise, more relaxed and open. We had breakfast and then talked. I was amazed at Diane's ability to get through stuff and encouraged by the fact that we could go through such a dark night of the soul and come out the other side as not only deeper friends but affectionate with each other as well.

It was a real testament to telling the naked truth. And once again, I was hopeful that maybe, just maybe, we could actually create what we both desired—a loving, awake partnership.

Diane ⌒

After our talk, I made him hug me and he resisted a tiny bit, but we laughed about it. Then I gave him space, got his lunch ready for him and said goodbye, not reaching out again for him. He pulled me close and kissed me, then kissed me again, then said, *"now don't get all gooey with me."*

But I came right back at him, *"You like it that I'm like that, when you're open, and you know it."*

He laughed and said, *"You're right."*

Things were on a good note, a real miracle, considering what we'd gone through just a few hours before.

Chapter 7

Soaring Free, Finding the Updrafts

"A heart to love, and in that heart, courage..."

- Shakespeare

Diane ⌣

After he left, I looked forward to spending the day alone, till mid afternoon. I wrote again, calming myself. Through email, I reached out, across the planet to a few close girlfriends, sharing what I'd gone through the night before. One of them wrote right back, furious and upset and telling me to get out for sure. The other one reflected my other feelings, to stay centered and ride it out. The two mirrored my own inner turmoil, but even in the midst of it all, I felt open, alive and good.

I toured the tiny village on the bike, took a chilly dip in the lake, then pedaled the six miles out to the airfield, past rolling hills and open fields, to go up gliding with him. The airfield sat alongside a cow pasture and the cows munched and mooed as the light airplanes glided in and out nearby.

As I got strapped into the glider, I realized how much I trusted him, that even after what had happened the night before, I was willing to go up in the sky and soar around with him in a tiny, fragile looking plane, without an engine, without a question.

The tow plane pulled us down the field and then we lifted up into the sky, just the sound of the wind, no drone of an engine. We banked to the left and began to soar. All my life, I'd had dreams of flying and this felt pretty close, like we were riding mother nature, in sync with her moods and fancies, soaring, falling, circling, natural like a bird.

I thought about life, as I looked down on the green fields dotted with sheep below and the treetops we skimmed over. Gliding and life both required paying close attention to what was happening moment by moment—like this relationship I was in with the man flying the plane.

Where were the updrafts, with the wind beneath my wings, where I was carried by something larger than myself? And what was I supposed to learn in a down draft, with the ground coming up fast?

That day, we were in new, calmer territory between us. He seemed to realize that a little affection wouldn't kill him and I was giving him more room and not needing as much reassurance. We drove part of the way back to his house and camped one night along the ocean.

I woke up to rain pouring down, loud on the van and lay awake for an hour. I looked over at him sleeping next to me. My mind still argued loudly that I needed to find a man who was more loving, kind and warm. It had a definite point there, which I was considering. I held up my fingers to the campground light shining through the window to count the days left—*nine*.

But I had other thoughts too. That he had learned to be cold as a survival mechanism from his childhood. I knew about that behavior first hand—my mother had been cold and withholding to my father and to me. I'd learned to be like that too, as a defense against her.

But my father and sister had saved me with their warmth and love and I'd healed; I'd learned the healing power of being loving and generous, both for me and for the person I was expressing it to. Maybe that's why I hated his coldness so much—because I used to do that too and knew firsthand the cost of it.

In the morning, I told him he should go out and find a woman who totally fit his pictures, and see how that turned out.

"I've already done that, more than once," he answered.

"And what happened?" I asked.

"It never turned out," he admitted. Now that was interesting!

When I wrote that day, my inner guidance told me, *"This is a discovery process and journey for you. Trust the journey. Trust the depth. Trust the tenderness. Stay deep, stay strong, stay beautiful. You can."*

That felt encouraging. I was glad that *someone* was sure, even if it was the mysterious voice inside of me.

Back at his house, I spent the day alone on his property, unpacking and washing clothes, then hanging them out to dry. I felt tender as I hung up his t-shirts, imagining his shoulders filling them out, feeling the intimacy of hanging up our laundry. I was hopelessly attached and feeling the rawness of that. But raw also felt very alive. It reminded me of the *Six-Day Course* I'd been in thirty years before, that he'd led—exhausting, confronting, terrible, and yet wonderful.

I went up to his bookshelf and chose two books on relationship. I like to hold a new book, ask for guidance, then open it at random and see what I am guided to read. The first book described how the author had discovered that he was "touch phobic." When his wife tried to be affectionate, he resisted it and felt uncomfortable. *"Wow, that sure sounds familiar!"* I thought.

The second book opened to a description of a process that the author had prescribed to his most difficult case—a couple that seemed hopelessly doomed to split up.

He told them to each write a list of things they used to do for each other when they were first in love. Then they had to start doing those things again, but they could only be done as a gift. In other words, he was asking them to bypass their minds completely, the minds that were busy arguing, the minds that had caused them to fall out of love.

When Landon got home later that afternoon, I shared with him what I'd found in the books. He agreed that he was touch phobic and said I could touch him all I wanted, and he would just deal with his reactions if they arose—in other words, I didn't have to stop.

That felt like a huge liberation for me, to know that he wouldn't be judging me as "needy" or "clingy" if I wanted to connect with him by touching him. It helped me to relax more around the issue too and to feel more accepted.

We talked about the assignment from the second book, the lists. Since we didn't have a history of being "first in love," we decided to make lists of things we'd like the other to do for us. After dinner, we wrote out our lists, then shared them with each other.

My list had twenty-two items that all involved connecting with him. His list had seven items, five of which involved having space from me and no connection. We had to laugh about it—the differences were so drastic.

We had a deep, close evening and night together and I felt more hopeful. I realized that I hadn't spent this much time alone with anyone, let alone a man I was involved with so intensely, in many years. We were on new ground that felt more stable. And yet as we got closer, we got deeper, bringing up more wounds that needed to be healed.

From my writing and meditation, I realized that my job was to stand in my light, no matter what was happening around me. If I could do this with the most vulnerable places in my heart, I could do it with anything.

I was still dealing with the pain of his criticism. He either wouldn't look at me, afraid he wouldn't like what he saw or when he did look at me, he'd see my wrinkles or that I wasn't thin enough. He couldn't see the good in me. But I was discovering that I deserve to be seen and to be loved, not criticized.

The next morning, I told him, *"All those things you think that you like in women, those are all just pictures from the past, keeping you from being in the real present, in life and with me. They keep you safe. You don't see me, my goodness, my beauty and my worth and that is not alright with me."*

"I deserve to be loved deeply and tenderly and if you are not able and willing to do that, at the end of this 'experiment,' I am going to find someone who will."

I meant it. He listened.

Landon ⌒

As the intimacy between us drove up our patterns and wounds, all we could do was start where we were—upset— and try to talk our way to the other side, and to, hopefully, more freedom.

I was starting to see that my attraction to other women or my inability to see Diane as beautiful caused an upset in my otherwise joyous experience of being with her. I really liked Diane for who she was, courageous, kind, loving, open, and responsible. And the more times I *did* see her as young, vibrant and beautiful, especially when we were making love or when I would catch a glimpse of her walking across the yard or in a moment of excitement about her work, the more painful it was for both of us when I *didn't* see her as beautiful.

I was afraid that when I couldn't see her beauty it was a message that we should not be together. Or that I was not able to authentically give Diane what she wanted and deserved—to be totally loved and fully appreciated. This felt uncomfortable and I suffered, resisting how I sometimes perceived her and wishing for a different perception.

I would often just not look at her, afraid of what I would see and not wanting to see her as "not beautiful." This triggered her pattern of "being invisible"—a deep wound from her growing up as the youngest of four with a mother who was not very motherly!

So our patterns fit together perfectly to be able to reveal (and hopefully heal) the early childhood wounds, but first we had to go through being upset!

I understood how perception functioned and had written extensively about it in my earlier book, *Living Awake*. I knew that beauty was in the eye of the beholder as I had often seen myself in the mirror, sometimes looking really good and sometimes looking old and ugly.

My perception of myself seemed to be dependent on how I felt about myself. Was I feeling OK about myself or was I feeling Not OK about myself because I hadn't exercised, or wasn't being productive, or I was discouraged by the pain in my ankles, etc.? It seemed that how I saw myself was a function of how I felt about myself.

So using this as a foundation, I started exploring whether the same dynamic might be true with Diane. Was I not feeling good about myself and projecting that perceptive filter onto Diane? Or was my perception of her as not attractive actually a message from the universe that Diane was not my partner?

More than a year later, I would understand that it all started with my pattern of "this isn't it" and I therefore had to see Diane as "not beautiful" so she wouldn't be "it," the evidence reconfirming my original declaration stemming from birth. But at the time I was trying to figure out what was going on and trying to get my experience to line up with my desire to see Diane's beauty. In the meantime we both suffered.

What kept me hanging in there and coming back was a deep sense that I had found a truly great partner for the path I had chosen to freedom. A path that required brutal honesty and truth telling and an opening to a love so deep that its vulnerability would bring up all the patterns and upsets that kept us from being free.

Also, I liked everything that we experienced together including the challenging talks to explore the structure of our own minds and our ego's apparent desire to ruin our good experiences by creating upsets.

The looks thing seemed to be the only impediment, but that was starting to wear away. At first I hadn't wanted to be seen in public together as a "couple," especially showing affection as Diane liked to do. But then I saw photos of us and saw that we did look good together and other people would also comment that we made a striking couple.

Chapter 8

The Journey Continues

"Love can't give you everything,
but it gives you what you need..."

- Kate Wolf, *Give Yourself to Love*

Diane ⌒

We were coming to the end of the "nineteen-day experiment" and were sharing a level of depth and intimacy that I'd never felt before. It was where I thought we'd be when I'd arrived, but at least we got there by the end. He asked me if I could see myself there in New Zealand and I said yes, for part of the year, for sure. That felt like a glimpse of a possible future, just for a second.

But he still seemed unsure. As he left one day, he looked back, smiled and said: *"I love you. It feels pretty smooth here..."* and he made a motion with his arms like waves. That felt so tender and lovely. Then he added, *"but no promises"* and held up his hands like two stop signs. *Ugh.*

That day, as I considered what we'd been through in *"the experiment,"* I realized that even if it ended, I was happy at the growth I'd experienced, and at the strength I'd discovered in myself. Thinking about all I'd been through with him, I wrote, *this is why I came here, to find out that I could stand in the center of the flames and not get burned.*

When I told him, he was excited. *"If you discovered that, then I'm really happy for you. That's what I would have wished for you."* It did feel great. I was not the same person who had landed there two and a half weeks before. I could face whatever came and let go if I needed to.

The day before we left, we went shopping in the little town of Takaka, the town closest to his home. I had some time on my own and browsed the shops and stores. In one, I found a lovely green summery top and went into the dressing room to try it on.

After all the days of swimming at the beach, long bike rides and sunshine, I was slim and tan. As I tried on the top, I thought to myself, *"I really am pretty! If he can't see it, then he is just blind."* That felt so good, to see my own beauty, in spite of his criticisms.

When I'd planned my trip to New Zealand, I'd booked myself on the same return flight to San Francisco as Landon. So we were going to be traveling together on the long journey back to California.

He had to find someone to drive his van the two and a half hour drive back from the Nelson airport to his home. It ended up that his ex-girlfriend Julie, the one he'd had really good sex with, was going to drive over with us and then bring the van back.

As I watched these plans come together and listened to their animated phone conversations, I felt pangs of jealousy and insecurity. *Oh no, just rub salt into my wounds, why don't you? I'm just starting to feel okay here and now I have to ride with her all the way to the airport?* Would the challenges never end with this man?

In the busy hours before our departure, I didn't tell him how I felt—I was embarrassed about my insecurity and he was distracted with all the preparations to leave. I was also going through my own feelings about leaving—I'd loved my time in New Zealand, in spite of all the emotional turmoil, and wasn't sure if I would ever be coming back. I kept remembering that our agreement and the "experiment" would end after the long flight.

As we drove over to Julie's house, the beauty of the landscape passed by the van window—the sparkling blue ocean, the woolly sheep grazing in green meadows, the tiny town of Takaka, with the health food store, boutiques and little café—but I barely saw it.

We pulled up to Julie's house and I got out of the car, bracing myself. But then she walked up and smiled and I relaxed. Since I'd lost my sister, I so appreciated women with whom I felt a rapport and from the first moment I met Julie, she felt like a sister. Julie had a boyfriend who was riding along too, so he and Landon sat in the front and Julie and I sat in the back.

Landon announced, *"You can talk about me, I don't care."* So we did just that. I was curious to hear her side of the story—he'd told me that she had ended the relationship. But that was not how she saw it—he'd been the one to end the relationship. Now *that* was interesting.

I told her some of what he'd put me through and she was sympathetic. We talked non-stop for the two and a half-hour drive. When we hugged goodbye, she told him, *"You'd be crazy to let her go."* I thought so too.

As we waited to get onto the plane, I told him, *"She was someone you chose, who you saw across the room, who fit your pictures, was over twenty years younger than you, and she still wasn't it. There is just no hope in this conversation with you."* It was the truth and he knew it and it felt good to stand up to him.

As we settled into our seats on the plane, I asked him to say something to connect before we went to sleep and he said, *"I like you and am glad that you're my friend."* After the closeness we'd shared, that felt like a slap in the face and I told him that wasn't enough for me. I was ready to bail again. Then over the long hours of the flight, seeing his long, lean body scrunched into the tiny economy seat as he twisted and turned trying to sleep, I felt tender towards him again. I rubbed his back and softened.

Landon ᴖ

Being with Diane had started an ongoing inquiry into the nature of love. I wasn't having my normal feelings of what I thought love was (all the indicators I had used in the past that initiated my going after some woman and which told me, "I am in love with this person").

On one hand, what Diane and I shared, when it was good, was the best I could imagine it being and kept getting better. Yet on the other hand, a lifetime of all my old indicators were not lining up. And this time around I had promised myself "no compromises." My thoughts and emotions had to be consistent and fully integrated for me to commit.

The inquiry went something like this. *So what is love in an intimate relationship? Is it the feelings of wanting, the desire to possess this other person? Is it a male ego enhancement as I help out this needy damsel in distress?* (I had played that role more than once.) *Is love the sense of wanting to nurture, care for, or protect another? Is it that I miss her when she is gone, or worry about her if she is late? Or is it just two people with similar insecurities attracting one another for healing—kind of an applied law of attraction with some sexual juice thrown in? Does love have form as in a specific set of experiences or is love formless?*

These questions kept me on the fence and made me hesitant to surrender to the love I *did* feel at times and to commit for a longer term. Therefore when Diane would ask me for some validation of our connection, I took great pains to only say what was true for me at that moment. At least in that way I was being authentic and she would then know that when I did say something complimentary, it was my real experience.

In the airplane, beginning our long flight, what I said—that I liked her and was glad she was my friend—was how I was feeling at that moment.

Diane ⌒

When we landed in San Francisco, the "nineteen-day experiment" was officially over, with no further commitment. He could just walk away—and so could I. On the Airporter bus ride to pick up my car, my mind was screaming again. *Get out now because he is just going to put you through this over and over again.*

I told him what it was saying. But when I dropped him off at his car, he gave me luscious kisses and promised to come up the next night. When he acted loving and warm like that, I felt so connected, good and happy.

He called later that day, after he'd told his friend what we'd gone through during my visit. *"I told him how brave you are, that you are able to handle all the stuff that comes up with me. I love you."*

He was coming up the next day and I felt excited and happy. Could we finally be getting to the good part of this love story?

We'd see what the Divine had in mind.

I called him once to check in before he came and could feel his coolness. *Oh no, not again. This is just too much.* And that wasn't just my mind. It *was* becoming too much. There is a phrase in French *"ça suffit"* which means *"that's enough,"* emphatically. I was getting close to emphatic and enough.

I asked him where he was in the "open" or "closed" department. He said "medium." I felt kind of neutral. *We'll see,* I thought.

When he arrived, he acted guarded, but I just met him and let him sleep off some of the jet lag. I'd fixed a delicious dinner, with candles and soft music. When we sat down at the table, he still had not warmed up and seemed to be avoiding looking at me. That was it for me.

"You're on thin ice here. Why did you even come if you were going to act this way? Don't waste my time."

And the great part was that I meant it. I was ready to walk away from this person who couldn't make up his mind.

He told me that he was worried that he hadn't gotten a solid *"yes"* about me. Listening to his fears, I calmed down again. *This was just another layer to be cleared out, it seemed.*

I suggested that as long as it wasn't a solid *"no"* for either of us, why didn't we extend the experiment for a few weeks longer? And not to worry about the solid *"yes."* If we were still in "the experiment" that also gave me an out, if he kept being cold and wishy-washy. The energy felt light and good again.

Landon ⌒

Diane's brilliant idea, *if it is not a definite "no" then it doesn't have to be a definite "yes,"* put my mind at ease and allowed me to be more in the moment, building my memory bank of positive shared experiences. For me the "no commitment" part of the "nineteen-day experiment" had been an important aspect of the equation and now I had a similar way of handling my mind's constant questioning of every little experience "does this mean she is it or not?"

I had calmed my mind in a similar way in a previous relationship when my partner kept saying, "I'm not sure you're my man" and I would say, "why don't we put that question on hold for six months?" We would then have an easier time of it, without the pressure on every moment.

With this problem out of the way with Diane, I could relax and open up to the reality of being with her at her home— cozy candlelight dinners, making love by the fire and deep intimate talks.

Diane ⌣‿

That evening, as Landon and I sat across the table from each other in the candlelight, he was talking about his relationship with his mother, then went on to another topic.

"No, go back, there is more there," I said, sensing something big.

He sat up and looked, trusting my sense, then started talking about how he felt, at thirteen months of age, when his brother was born. (He had accessed this in the past through regression therapy.) Then he saw it.

"I decided to withhold from women and to reject them, because that seemed to be what my mother was doing with me." We both sat, stunned at the significance of what he had just uncovered.

Then he saw another piece, *"I am really hard on myself, so being hard on you is a defense and a way to be 'better' than you."* Wow, another piece of ego machinery being exposed.

As we continued to talk in the new open space, I told him that it took the deep intimacy and connection that we shared to drive up the hidden wounds and those depths can only be reached with a partner. He agreed.

"I love you, Diane. Thank you for being my angel." I let those words in to soothe my heart and soul.

I was leaving on a trip the next day and we were going to be apart for six days. When we said goodbye, it felt close and deep. Could we stay there this time?

We talked on the phone each day and he stayed warm and loving. He was going to spend one night alone at my farm, then I was coming back the next day in the afternoon. We'd just have a few hours together, before he had to leave that evening to drive back to San Francisco.

As the days passed, he didn't close down.

"Thank you for being so courageous. You can look forward to me being open," he promised.

I could feel his open heart, even from five hundred miles away, so I got up at five in the morning and paid a hundred and fifty dollar fee to change my flight, to have three extra hours with him that day before he had to leave.

When I arrived home, he welcomed me with a big hug and kiss. We spent the whole day talking, making love and snuggling in front of the fire as rain poured down outside. He was how I'd always known he could be, open and loving, like a wall had come down.

Being alone in my home had been powerful for him. He'd even looked at a photo of me from thirty years before, when my daughters were young, that before he hadn't liked. This time when he looked at the picture, he could see that I was pretty. That got his attention. Clearly the photo hadn't changed; his perception of it had changed.

At one point in our afternoon together, he went out to his car to get a song he wanted to share with me, "Go where love goes," sung by Andrea Bocelli, and we listened to it together.

Go where love goes
Go where your heart leads
Angels are pleading with you
Go there
Go where love dares to go...

He told me that the first time he heard it, he had wept.

He invited me to go to New York with him in April, where he was leading a seminar. And then on to North Carolina, to meet family, including his ninety-year-old mother, Peggy.

I was thrilled, taking deep breaths to relax and open to the new space we were in, the one I'd felt was possible from the beginning. Could this really be happening?

Yes, it was, a new space of love and partnership. He left that evening, promising to come back as soon as he could.

Then sweet phone calls over the days apart. *"You're everything I've been looking for,"* he said.

Landon ⌒

When I went up to Diane's house to spend the night alone, it felt powerful to take in the space by myself—her cozy home set back on eight acres, with the rock fireplace, wood floors and views of trees out of every window. I could feel her there, in all her touches, the tablecloths and candles, the pictures of her and her children at different ages.

I stood in front of a photo of Diane and her daughters from thirty years before. As I gazed at it, I was thinking, "would I have liked her when she was younger?" I had looked at that picture specifically at an earlier time with the same question on my mind and had not found her particularly attractive. Now as I looked again, I saw how beautiful she was. I felt amazed—the photo hadn't changed, just my perception of it had.

I slept alone in her bed and woke up still filled with the sense of wonder that my own unexamined filters had kept me from seeing her beauty all that time. I was excited that she was coming back earlier to give us more time together before I had to leave again and I was feeling more open and willing to express my love for her.

Chapter 9

Opening to a New Life

*"Trust, more than ever, the strength of softness,
tenderness, vulnerability."*

- Diane's inner guidance

Diane ⌒

I was beginning to live what I had always known was possible, a space of love, magic, creativity, freedom, and deep peace. I could feel the power of having unraveled places where we'd been entangled by the mind and ego, both individually and together.

After he left that day, we stayed connected over the phone with intimate, long talks. *"Thank you for loving me so that I could begin to love myself,"* he said. I knew that loving him was something that I could not help—even at the times when I didn't like him, I couldn't turn away.

I flew to San Diego to meet him for a rowing regatta he was competing in. I treasured meeting all his friends and being introduced as his partner.

After the races, we drove north to meet both of my daughters and their families, which felt easy and good. We looked ahead to twenty-four days together until he had to leave again, the longest time we'd spent without a break. What would it be like to share our newfound intimacy for three and a half weeks?

We headed up the coast, happy to be alone and free. I'd planned a special birthday celebration for him that included camping one night in Big Sur, one night at an inn there and a day at Esalen Institute, one of my favorite places on the planet.

The roads were deserted that early spring morning as we drove up windy Highway One towards Big Sur. We stopped several times to take in the magnificent scenery—the waves pounding against the steep cliffs, the green hills, the fresh, crisp ocean air, with seagulls diving and calling.

We camped in Big Sur, cozy in the van, as rain pounded down. Then our day at Esalen Institute, soaking in the mineral baths and eating the sumptuous organic food was perfect—fun and relaxing. That night, after dinner, we stayed at an old, cozy inn just up the road and celebrated his birthday.

There was an ease now between us. We laughed and talked in the car as we drove the next afternoon along the coastal road north. It felt so good to look back on all that we'd gone through, to see it in the past and to relish the present. The future felt wide open and we both felt the peace and happiness of looking forward together.

"See, it turned out—what you ran away from at first, that I liked you so much. Maybe no one has ever liked you as much as I have." I teased him.

"Probably not. You're the best person I've found on the planet for doing relationship with," he said.

We were in a magical space of new love, not based on fantasy, but on authentic connection and communication.

A few days later, as we waited at the San Francisco airport to board our plane to New York, I couldn't help remembering the last time I was there with him, when we returned from New Zealand, just one month earlier, when I'd been ready to give up.

So much had happened since then, and our relationship was so much deeper and more certain. When I told him what I was thinking, he smiled and told me I looked beautiful. I put my head on his shoulder, feeling content and grateful.

We spent five days in New York, as he taught his three-day seminar, *The Essence of Personal Mastery.* On the first day, he shared about our relationship and the journey we'd been on and introduced me. At one point, on the second day, one of the participants raised his hand and turned and pointed to me.

"We want to hear more from her." Landon laughed and then invited me to come up to the front. That was a magical moment, to see that what I'd gone through with him, withstanding his resistance and staying committed to what I knew was real, even in the face of my own mind screaming—that my experience contributed to others.

I could feel the power of it reflected in their faces, eager to hear more. They wanted to believe that there was a way through the pain and morass of relationship troubles and that their dreams of love could also come true. That they could withstand the torment of their own mind to stay in with someone they loved, even when it was painful.

He led a powerful seminar, I made a real contribution to it and the participants left happy and satisfied. Our last day in New York, we walked in Central Park, looked in the window at Tiffany's, checked out the lobby of the Waldorf Astoria, where he'd stayed with his grandmother years before, and had fun being tourists.

Then we flew to North Carolina to meet his family—his mother, his brother and his brother's wife. I loved being his partner, in the inner circle of his family. I kept pinching myself and taking deep breaths. *Yes, this was real. No, I wasn't imagining it. Yes, he was still warm and loving.*

When we flew back to California, we had five days before he left again for New Zealand for a month. At the back of my mind, haunted by the previous two times he'd gone back, I had a nagging worry that he would withdraw again.

But I had to trust, stay strong and keep believing in what we had now. When he returned, in May, he was going to move in with me. Then, if all went well, we would go back to New Zealand together, in the winter, seven months later.

He never asked me, *"What do you think about me moving in with you?"* It was just accepted that he would. It felt right and I continued to trust that.

I felt so new and different, and my life, at age sixty-one, was new and different, with a man I loved, with every fiber of my being. He'd challenged us to be unreasonable so many years ago in the *Six-Day Course.* With this relationship, I'd been unreasonable, was still being unreasonable and it was amazing.

Before he left, as we lay by the fire together, he said, *"I have a huge amount of gratitude, to have you in my life, to know that I love you and to have this part of my life together."*

"When you come back, you'll get to have the summer you didn't have last year—the sun, the river and me," I said as we said goodbye. He laughed. I stood and watched him drive down the driveway, feeling full, peaceful and loved.

That night, I thought of him flying through the dark, open, sky, carrying my love in his heart. We had moved through so many spaces since the beginning and then again, since he spent the night alone in my home, just five weeks before. I listened to his special song, "Go where love goes," and felt moved and tender as I crawled into bed to sleep alone for the first time in weeks.

In the days and weeks ahead, we emailed and talked often, maintaining the intimacy we'd established. He stayed open and warm, calling me *sweetheart* and *darling*. A pair of wild geese landed in my apple orchard and stayed for a few days. I had read that the beautiful, elegant birds mated for life. They stayed close together, never out of each other's sight.

I remembered taking walks with my sister Sharon before she got sick, when we would hear the wild geese calling to each other in their throaty, haunting call. We would stop and gaze up at them in wonder as they flew in their V formation high in the sky.

So it felt like a "love blessing", from my sister, from the farm and from the universe, to have this pair of geese visit the farm, just before Landon came back to live with me.

As the weeks passed, I noticed that my mind was busy, coming up with fears about the relationship, that we *wouldn't* stay connected and then, at some deep level, that we *would* stay connected. It seems that it was so addicted to problems and upsets, that it wanted the relationship to fail so that it could be right and separate. It had *liked* the drama of the ups and downs, the ins and outs, maybe because it was familiar and similar to the pain with my mother, of not feeling loved or good enough? It was afraid either way it turned out!

But I was onto it. I wrote, *we're in love here, deep, awake, pure and good love and we're connected. Separate is so over.*

As I was driving, my inner guidance felt so powerful and wise that I pulled over and wrote it down. *"You were strong in his 'not love.' Now be strong in his 'love.' You were strong in his 'not accepting.' Now be strong in his 'accepting.' You were strong in his 'you are not my partner.' Now be strong in his 'you are my partner.'"*

There was so much truth in that. It was like I had to break up the hard places around my heart to receive his love. I had found a way to love him and to stay tender. But this was new territory—being loved in return.

He would be gone for four weeks, a total of twenty-eight days. I was counting them off, one by one. If I hadn't committed to teaching writing classes, I'd have gotten on a plane and gone to be with him. As winter turned to spring, it was as if I could feel my own heart thawing out after a long freeze.

The voice still talked to me, especially when I was first waking up in the morning. *"Peace, love, joy and depth, laughter and celebration. You have waited a very long time, so enjoy it all now."* I let those words sink in as I lay there, opening up to the new day.

As the hours and days counted down, we stayed connected, energetically, across the planet. I used the time to prepare on the inner and the outer plane, cleaning up the house and farm, writing in my journal. The voice kept encouraging me:

"Trust, more than ever, the strength of softness, tenderness, vulnerability. Know that you are ready for this. Keep saying—'I am ready. I am ready to receive all this good and all these blessings.'"

He was going to be living here with me. Those four words, *living here with me* rocked my world. Who I really was embraced it with ease. But the old me was trying to catch up, huffing and puffing from the exertion. Would she ever catch up? Was there a bridge between the two? Did I just ignore her—she got me to where I was, so I was grateful to her.

I wanted the transition to go easily, tenderly, softly, the way the buds in spring were opening up all over the farm from the new warmth of the sun.

I hadn't lived with a man for thirty years. I had a life and he had a life and now there was going to be "our life" and that would be the new territory.

I had become balanced in my own male/femaleness, but now, we could discover the magical polarity of man/woman, male/female and explore that together in day-to-day life.

There was no room in my old life for any of my new life to fit—his moving in, my work and writing, the farm, family and friends. I could see that I needed to stand in my new life and not look back.

The voice said, *"Stay strong. Believe in yourself."* I listened.

I told him on the phone that we could have a really fun summer—be like wild teenagers, going to the river, sleeping outside, playing and having fun. We both were excited to begin our new life and to being together, for the rest of the year and beyond.

"Just be present with him. Just love him," the voice said. I could do that. I would do that.

Chapter 10

Follow Your Bliss

"Trust that you are growing and
changing at a rate and in ways you could not do on our own."

- Diane's inner guidance

Diane ⌒

Landon arrived late in the evening, tired from his long hours of travel. I put him to bed and had some time to myself. I didn't feel as connected as I had, but thought that could just take some time.

I'd noticed that I'd been tuning out my mind, just hearing it as static, not even distinguishing the thoughts, like a TV in the background, droning on. Or a maiden aunt who always gave the doomsday report and you'd think, *just be kind to her but don't pay any attention to her words.*

But as the first few days unfolded, he admitted that when he got out of the car and saw me, his mind told him he was trapped. It took him a day and a half of being reserved to open up and tell me and during those days, I suffered.

My mind yelled, *That's it, I'm done. Tell him to go find another woman to do this drama with.* Forget my mind just being "static." Those words and feelings came through loud and clear.

I tried to stay calm. It took us five challenging days of talking and looking to regain the ground we'd had before he left. As always, all my deepest fears were coming up—that I was not good enough, or else he would not have felt trapped. I hated that I still had those wounds.

"I love you, even when I don't think I do," I told him. The absurdity of that made me laugh, which helped.

"I'm not going anywhere," he said. That helped too.

During the first days and weeks of living together, he still struggled with being attracted to women he saw in the grocery store or on the street and would admit those feelings after being closed down and withdrawn. I tried to keep a perspective when my mind was wailing—*why am I doing this?*

"Just weather the storm and don't lose sight of the truth of who you really are, no matter what your mind says," the voice said. I clung to those wise words and held on.

Landon ⌣⤳

I had moved in with Diane at her lovely farm in Nevada City, California. While I had a whole life back in New Zealand, it felt quite natural to "go for it one hundred percent" because how else were we going to find out if we were true partners? I looked forward to the reality of this new life and the ease of day-to-day living with Diane, a rowing lake just ten minutes up the road, good biking and, *"Two cats in the yard... now everything is easy, cuz of you"* ("Our House" a Crosby, Stills, Nash and Young song).

My only concern was that I *still* kept getting hooked by being attracted to other women. I interpreted that as either Diane wasn't "it" or that I could not fully commit because I must not be one hundred percent certain. In any regard, it still pained me and I was reluctant to keep bringing it up to Diane, as it hurt and upset her. Then I would make myself wrong for having "wandering thoughts," feel ashamed and "not good enough" (one of my primary declarations about myself I formulated as a child) and withdraw and withhold those thoughts.

This would lead to Diane feeling my withdrawn coldness and she would feel "invisible" and judged and "not good enough," so we would have an upset on our hands anyway! She would break the ice by saying, *"What's going on?"* and I would reluctantly admit to some passing attraction to a girl who probably should have been a model for Victoria's Secret catalog—young, skinny and blonde!

But all this was necessary for me to discover the enslaving machinery of my mind and its workings. For in the face of real, deep, love, my mind/ego, which had said all along "I want deep love," was doing everything in its power to prevent me from having it.

I knew intellectually that the mind is addicted to *wanting*, not having, because getting what we want ends the game of *wanting*. And I knew that the mind/ego thrives on not having, incompleteness, and dissatisfaction, because that feeds the *wanting*. My ego, in its effort to preserve itself, seemed only too willing to rob me of the satisfaction and happiness I had been searching for virtually my whole life. I realized once again that for the most part, my mind is not my friend.

As Diane's and my love grew deeper, my ego used every aspect of my most fundamental declarations about myself (this isn't it, I am separate, and I am not good enough) to try and counter what was happening and preserve the ego identity of *Landon*.

In each case, I would first be lost in the evidence that appeared *soooo real* and lose sight of the context from which the evidence arose. For example, I would *really* feel depressed and down, reinforcing "I am not good enough or not OK," or Diane would *really* not look beautiful or I would really see a woman I was attracted to which reinforced "my current circumstance isn't it."

I was lost in the illusion of forms, believing the evidence as real; I mean, "there it was, it *really* happened, I *really* experienced it!" I had failed to stay awake to the full truth of what was going on inside me, both the experiences <u>and</u> the context from which they arose. I was giving my power to choose to the illusion and becoming a victim of my mind's interpretation that *in fact,* "this isn't it, and I'm not good enough."

In a regression experience about my birth, I had remembered being alone without my mother, who was drugged and recovering, and the nurse being callous in her handling of weighing me on a cold scale.

In addition, the blanket they put around me irritated my skin, I was hungry and felt trapped in this little body—not a pleasant experience! I decided in a non-verbal way *"this can't be what life on earth was supposed to be!"* And somehow, *"I wasn't enough"* or all of that wouldn't have happened.

I had lived within the terrible domination of both of these contextual declarations (this isn't it and I'm not good enough) all my life and firmly believed them to be true. In fact they were two of the core beliefs or foundations of my identity as Landon. In spite of an outward appearance of success and well-honed social skills, I lived with an ever-present undercurrent of unhappiness and dissatisfaction. But at the time, I was still working my way up through the layers of unconsciousness about this deep programming.

As painful as it was to talk about my attraction to other women with Diane and to see how much that upset her, when we each talked about our individual experiences responsibly, we brought them out of the darkness and into the light of consciousness. That diminished another piece of the mind's hold on us and created more freedom to experience the joy and relatedness that we wanted. Each time we healed an upset, it validated the old adage "the truth shall set you free." And we were both committed to that freedom.

Diane ⌒⌐

Landon left to fly back east for his Yale college reunion and I relished the space to try to regain my balance. Being apart gave us both some perspective. I realized that, at some level, I had known that by being in a relationship with him, all the places I needed to heal would surface. Even though my mind screamed, wanting to protect those wounds, my true self, that desired freedom, wanted to heal them. And that is what we were doing.

When Landon returned, we did better at navigating the issues as they came up. Things calmed down and took on a new depth and richness.

It was summer now and we lived outside, sleeping, showering and eating out on the deck. I could feel myself opening up to "day-to-day love," expressed in making morning shakes, cooking dinners together, washing our clothes and hanging them on the line, making him a plate for lunch when I made one for myself; his buying groceries and printer cartridges and taking the trash down to the road. Sleeping out under the giant oaks, we woke tangled up together when the birds started to sing, just before the sun rose.

"It was grand," as my Dad would have said.

One night, as we lay under the oaks, snuggled together, Landon admitted he was afraid of falling in love. He still had the pattern of closing down and withdrawing after we'd been especially intimate. I longed to be unaffected by his moods. I suggested that we'd had the "nineteen-day experiment." Why didn't we have the "seven-month experiment of falling in love?" That felt light and good and we both agreed to it.

Landon ⌒

I knew I wanted to be madly in love with Diane, but I didn't know how to do it. If I couldn't arrive there, then perhaps this really wasn't the relationship for me as neither of us would get what we wanted. So the *"seven-month experiment of falling in love"* seemed like a natural extension of what we had already been doing; at first *"stay in the relationship as long as the magic lasts,"* then the *"nineteen-day experiment in New Zealand"* followed by the *"if it's not a definite 'no' then it doesn't have to be a definite 'yes,'"* to now an experiment to see if I could fall in love.

While I wouldn't yet consider commitment, and didn't want to even talk about marriage, I thought that if I was going to live with

Diane, I needed my own space—a cave to go to. So that summer with a friend of Diane's who was a better carpenter than me, I converted part of an old shed of Diane's into an office for me and named it *"Landon's Den"* with the picture of my spirit animal, a wolf, on the sign.

I figured I could walk away from the money it cost me and it would be my parting contribution to Diane's farm. I was fooling myself as it turned out, but at the time that was my thinking and it allowed me to get what worked for me and justify the expense without saying I was *really* committed!

Diane ⁓

I flew to Southern California for the weekend to take care of my granddaughters. The space apart again felt good to get some perspective. I realized that I'd never let a man in this far before and the openness and risk of it felt uncomfortable. As I awoke, the voice was there, encouraging me. *"Trust that you are growing and changing at a rate and in ways you could not do on our own."*

I could see that in my new life with him, I was not *safe*, in the sense that the mind wanted to be. And that was good. But I was experiencing a kind of terror, being on such unfamiliar ground.

That morning, I took my granddaughters to a "fun zone" where they had tethered bungee jumping. It was something I'd watched the girls do many times, but had been afraid to try. That day, I decided to do it to break through my fears.

It was fun and freeing, scary and exciting. I screamed so loudly that when I was done, a crowd had formed to find out what all the commotion was about. My granddaughters cheered.

Later, at the beach, as we jumped through the waves and boogie boarded, laughing and playing, I noticed that I felt more happy, fulfilled and complete than I'd ever felt.

The space apart gave me some clarity. We'd been in the *"nineteen-day experiment,"* and now it was the *"seven-month adventure of falling in love."* We should *expect* things to come up—we were *living* together. How could they not?

We were flying east to visit family and friends and then to lead a relationship course together in New Jersey. The first leg of the trip, we visited his mother for nine days. That might have brought up unresolved pain from his childhood—he seemed extra critical and negative.

One night, out at a play, he ignored me, acting like we weren't together. Later, when I talked to him about it, he accused me of being needy. I felt off center, being away from home and staying in a dark basement room that I found depressing. We struggled to find our connection there.

Landon ⌣ꜛ

I think I have always looked for what is wrong and tried to fix it, perhaps in an effort to be perfect or just from some male programming. I have used this dynamic to motivate myself to some formidable accomplishments, but the satisfaction that should have accompanied those accomplishments soon dissipated. Because the motivation came from a sense of incompleteness, eventually dissatisfaction always overcame the momentary high from what I'd accomplished.

If I look now, I can see the dynamic as just the methodology that would naturally come from a declaration of "this isn't it" and

"I'm not good enough." Because I had been "successful" using this methodology, it was difficult to realize the true cost to myself of continuing the "dissatisfaction game."

By way of example, in my sports, I have always looked to see what was wrong or what I wasn't doing efficiently and have worked really hard in my training to correct the error. I would always drive myself to harder and harder workouts and in the process this had paid off in achievements—varsity letters in three sports, pro offers, captaining teams, national championships in masters rowing, etc.

But my athletic achievements hadn't started with me being a star by any means. In fact, in first and second grade, I was always the last person chosen for whatever team, with the comment by the two choosing captains, *"Who will take Carter?"* This definitely reinforced my "not good enough" programming and became my driver to excel so as to be accepted and admired rather than shunned and rejected. This pattern was deeply ingrained in my makeup.

So when Diane would say, *"You just said something critical about me, but you can make it up to me by telling me something nice,"* I didn't know what to say. I had trained myself to acknowledge my students, when I taught in a business I had co-founded called *Active Learning,* but I was hopeless at acknowledging myself, thinking that giving myself a compliment was arrogant. And when I actually looked in response to Diane's request, I saw that when I complimented another, I felt diminished myself!

So I withheld complimenting Diane, feeling she was insecure and needy and trying to cover up her "not good enough" pattern with my compliments rather than confronting the pattern itself.

I thought that I, on the other hand, was fully independent and not needing compliments. I was highly dysfunctional in this area and having a hard time seeing it.

Chapter 11

A New Life

"Open up your hearts to the tears and laughter..."

- Kate Wolf, *Give Yourself to Love*

Diane ⌐

We flew to Maine to stay with a good friend in a cabin on an island, no electricity, no phones, no Internet, and a brisk fifteen-minute boat trip from the mainland. With all the majestic beauty of the island, I started to feel more centered again.

The voice said, *"Don't worry about what he says or how he acts. Just keep having amazing, powerful and real experiences together and that will take care of everything."*

That could have been a warning because he opened up once again about his considerations about me not "being his pictures." I was at the end of my rope. There, at the cabin off the coast of Maine, just days before we were to lead a relationship course together, I was in so much pain that I wanted to bail.

Again, I couldn't help notice that I was stranded in a place where it was impossible to escape! And the worse the pain got, the more isolated we seemed to be. This time we were on an island where the only way out was by a boat I didn't know how to drive.

When he and I sat down to talk, I agreed to be "in" till my birthday, four months away, mid November. But if he was still having the same issues then, I was done. He agreed. I felt huge relief knowing that there was a time limit to the pain I was in.

Landon ⌒⟲

We were on a beautiful island off the coast of Maine and once again the trapped feeling of being with Diane when she wasn't totally "it" resurfaced. As I write this, it seems so obvious that it was just another layer of the pattern of "this isn't it," but at the time it seemed so real. I was closed down, withdrawn, resisting being affectionate and generally a pain in the ass to be with. But I still could not see the deep and persistent pattern of "this isn't it" resurfacing once again. I was still getting it in layers.

So once again, setting a time limit, in this case, Diane's birthday four months away in November, gave my mind a way of handling the pain of the upset, as it wouldn't last forever. The time limit also allowed us to observe what was going on, tell the truth of our current experience and move more into present time. Every time we could get into the present moment, we had joyous experiences and a deep connection.

The joy and connection made it easier and easier to surrender to the reality of Diane and let go of the internal conversation of "whether or not she was it?" But my mind was still not done with it yet.

The inquiry that started to surface about this time was, *where do these images that I seem so attached to and victimized by come from? Are they really my choice now? And do I want to put my life energy into supporting those images?*

In the 1990's when I was confronting my male chauvinist attitudes at the insistence of my wife, I read a book by Naomi Wolf called *The Beauty Myth.* In it, the author described how the four hundred top models in the fashion industry set the beauty standard for the world of cosmetics, hair, fashion, fitness, and cosmetic surgery—"the look"—against which most women measure themselves.

If you encountered these rail thin models on the street, you'd rarely find them attractive. They only look good in print! Talk about unreal. But as a non-awake male, I too fell for that look and then proceeded to entrain my mind with every comparison I made when I was on the hunt looking for my next mate. I know it sounds primal and I think the "hunting" part really could link back to "cave men times" in the DNA of most males.

The second programming source came from masturbation to pictures of women in girlie magazines when I was a teenager. Because our sexuality is linked to the survival of the species, this highly charged mind/body experience implants these images deep into the subconscious. Earlier in my life, I had seen this and weaned myself away from having any kind of fantasies around sex, preferring the reality of what was occurring, but I am sure there was still some of that yearning for the *sex siren.*

"Yearning" seems key here, a tip off that the mind's/ego game was in play—wanting what it didn't have. The strange thing was that Diane and I were enjoying the love making of

our lives, and for me, she was my teenage fantasy come true—
willing and passionate. I was learning again that my mind is not
my friend!

Diane ⌒

We left the island to travel to New Jersey to lead the
relationship course. Leading it together brought up new
challenges. He was so used to being the seminar leader that
he didn't co-lead well. I had to interrupt him to make my own
contributions and by the end we were angry at each other.

But when we sat down to de-brief, as we expressed our
frustrations and listened to each other, we were able to see the
real value we had created for the participants. As it turned out,
two out of the ten went out and started relationships and got
married within a year of the course. Plus, a couple who had been
struggling and ready to split up, were still together a year later
and having their first child.

Back home after weeks of travel, we escaped down to the
river for a swim, then back to our deck to make love again, our
precious space under the stars. It was so good to be home.

We were close and good, but I still went into pain when he'd
tell me that he had thoughts about other women. Or when he'd say
that he loved many of my qualities, but didn't find me beautiful.
I'd had lots of self-esteem issues, but at least had always felt
attractive. But even that had gotten worn away. I began to doubt
my own beauty, and that made me angry.

*"I lived my whole life with a critical, harsh and cold mother.
But I'm done with that. I have a lot I want to accomplish with
what is left in my life and I need someone who will be supportive*

and loving as my partner. And if you can't be that, then it is time to say goodbye."

That night, he realized that he'd decided that to help people, you had to show them what was wrong, so they could correct it. And that comes across as a put down, as a criticism.

I prayed to Saint Michael.

"Just love him. That heals you both. He needs the healing more than you, but you are healing too." That calmed me down.

I reread my journal from the beginning of our relationship. It was important to feel the wonder of just how far we'd come, and to recognize that I had known from the beginning what we could have together, what we were having together now.

"You're the perfect woman for me," he said, later. I wanted to let it in and not let my mind take me to—*"but what about not finding me beautiful?"* It still wanted to cling to that.

The depth of my feelings for him were way beyond anything I'd ever felt before. In the "seven-month adventure of falling in love," he was finally opening up to falling in love, so I could too. I had been holding back and hadn't even realized it.

"You're pretty wonderful and I love you so much," he said. But then he closed off again. We were in bed on the deck. I lost it.

"You're in my bed, on my deck and you're cold. You need to stop this." It felt so good to stand up to him. He heard me, then said he'd like to start over.

So I said, *"Okay, get back out and get in again."* He did and we had a nice snuggle before going to sleep. He told me that when he was withdrawn, he was not feeling good about himself. I needed to remember that. Then I could reach out with compassion instead of getting upset.

The next day, at the river he said, *"This is heaven and you are a big part of the heaven."* It felt like we'd turned a corner somehow and were on a straightaway with smooth road ahead. Finally.

It had been an amazing summer—travel, family fun, the river, sleeping outside, camping and lots of breakthroughs between us.

But we still had "bumps." As our connection deepened, Landon seemed to resist our intimate times together, our "dates." That felt confusing to me—what was there to resist? I made him talk about it and it opened up, I hoped for good.

Landon ⌒⌐

We had already gone through the touch phobic layer of my pattern of isolation in New Zealand, (arising from my declaration "I am separate and alone in this world") and I had designated Diane as my "pleasure guru" with the caveat that she could touch me whenever she wanted. I would have to deal with my own resistance if it surfaced, and I would follow her lead in the pleasure department.

In the past, I had tried the ascetic route of sitting alone in a cave and did not find that a very fast road to enlightenment. I had read about *Tantra*—the path of pleasure—but I had my doubts about it, as it seemed too much like debauchery. Also I was worried that it would increase my attachments and I was fairly certain I needed to let go of all attachments for full enlightenment. Nevertheless, with Diane as my pleasure guru, I had agreed to follow her lead.

So on one of the afternoons in which we had decided to have a date, I was feeling tired and grumpy and not wanting to make love. I thought it was strange that I was resisting the wonderful pleasure that we experienced together. As we talked about it, I started by defending myself, saying I was tired and I shouldn't be obligated to have a date if I didn't want to. Diane agreed, saying she was putting no pressure on me, but perhaps I could keep looking.

As I looked deeper, I saw that I was really afraid that I would not be able to perform as well as the last time and then I would not fulfill her expectations, and she would be upset and I would be rejected—so why go there! It was just another layer of my "not good enough" pattern and I was projecting onto Diane the complementary role of being upset and rejecting me. After we talked and I could let go of the child's performance fear of not being good enough, we had a wonderful date with no pressure and lots of pleasure.

Once again it fascinated me that my mind would try and make a problem out of anything, even the good stuff!

Diane ⌒

In early September, we went to a cabin on a lake for five days, up in the mountains. As we drove the windy road to the lake, I said, *"We may never get married, but let's start having honeymoons."* He thought that was a great idea.

I'd been going to this cabin for years, to swim, read, write and rest, enjoying the solitude, but had dreamed of sharing the rustic space with a partner.

One night in the cabin, I looked across the room at his strong body sprawled across the old iron bed, in his black sweater and ripped jeans. He fit so perfectly into the experience of being there and yet added so much. All those years of being single had been to prepare for this, for him, for us. I was being "minded" after all.

We'd each been healing broken places—wings, hearts, trust. But now, with both of us more whole, what could we create together?

The previous year, I'd been preparing for the "Big Love." As I looked back, I wrote a note to that self, who had been so patient, yet full of longing, *Don't give up. He's coming and will have been so worth the wait.*

And he *had* been so worth the wait. In the intimacy we now shared, I was discovering new depths to the energetic exchange that lovemaking could be.

We spent afternoons making love, then lying close and talking. Then after a brisk swim in the chilly lake and a warm shower, we'd cook dinner with the camp stove on the picnic table in front of the cabin, as the sun set and the ospreys circled and dove for fish. Then the moon rose and the Milky Way shone and sparkled, reflecting on the lake as we snuggled into our cozy cabin for the night.

It felt like a true honeymoon—being joyous and complete together, and yet, because of all the work we'd done for the past ten months, with no worries about a time when "the honeymoon would be over." We'd already gone through the tough part. Now we could relax and celebrate.

"I'm so lucky to have found you and I'm madly in love with you," he said, during one of our afternoons of intimacy.

Landon ⌒

Those four days in the cabin by the beautiful mountain lake, gave me a new perspective of what was possible for us. When Diane said, "We may never get married, but let's start having honeymoons," my mind could relax and I could be one hundred percent committed and present with her for those four days. I think the intensity of that continuous commitment opened up a new dimension of depth for us both. We had already developed a foundation of trust with our truth telling, and now we could more fully let go into the pleasure and ecstasy of Being.

Diane ⌒

I'd been training all summer for the mini-triathlon that I'd done in 2000 and 2001, in my sister Sharon's honor, with her cheering me on. I'd decided to do it again to honor her memory and Landon had been coaching me on the biking, even buying me a shiny, red road bike.

The evening before the triathlon, he loaded up the car with all my gear, pumped up my bike tires, and fixed my shoelaces to make them easier to tighten quickly, duct taping them down. No man had been that kind to me since my dad. I was so touched.

The day of the race, he volunteered and cheered me on as I biked and ran by his station. I was ten years older than the last time I had done it, stronger in the biking, and completed the race eighteen minutes faster overall, even placing fourth in my age group! We celebrated that powerful result of our partnership.

Chapter 12

Expanding My World

"Say yes to love, laughter, light and life..."

- Diane's inner guidance

Diane ⌒

I discovered that I was eligible to become an Australian citizen, by descent; my mother became an American citizen when I was one. By some amazing fluke, I had a file with her birth, marriage and naturalization certificates—everything I needed to apply. I downloaded the application, copied all mom's papers, got an FBI clearance and a photo, then bundled it all off to Washington DC with a check for one hundred fifteen dollars.

In mid September, I received a certificate that I was now an Australian citizen; I had a dual citizenship with the US and Australia. That meant I could go in and out of New Zealand freely. With my citizenship official, I applied for and got an Australian passport.

I couldn't explain logically why I wanted to become Australian—maybe I was trying to capture a part of my mother that I couldn't have when she was alive? I'd contacted several of her cousins and was hoping to visit when Landon and I went back to New Zealand the next winter. It all felt like another piece of healing with my mother and that felt important in my relationship with Landon.

As September turned into October, Landon and I stayed connected, without upsets. Our energetic soul connection and day-to-day life felt like a rich, thick stew of love and tenderness. Sexually, I opened up to him more than I ever had with a man, creating even more joy and ecstasy in our lovemaking.

He left to travel back east for a conference and I went back to a life alone, like it used to be, except that my life was not at all like it used to be. I knew now the magic that could exist between two people, the force of something bigger than your own small life flowing through and connecting to another person.

As we approached our one-year anniversary, I marveled that he was sharing my life at the farm, our lives totally intertwined. The farm was where I had learned to love myself, where I had weathered my sister's death, some heartbreaks, financial challenges, a betrayal in business. The farm took it all in and helped me to turn those painful experiences into wisdom, growth and freedom.

And when Landon first came, he fit at the farm. At some level, he knew it and it scared him. At a deep level, I knew it and I turned towards it. I never turned away and I felt proud of that.

I love loving him with the richness of wisdom, age and experience, I wrote in my journal. We were living the most amazing love story.

We were deeper than we had ever been, open to each other energetically, riding the waves of ecstasy.

And yet, the depth brought up all that was left to release and heal. We had one last bump about his criticism of my looks. Such deep pain on my end, being seen through a filter of what was wrong with me, not what was right with me—how my mother had treated me.

Throughout my life, I'd had lots of self-confidence issues, but had felt confident about my looks. I'd been told I was attractive, pretty, even beautiful. He was the first man who had told me he didn't find me attractive. Yes, I was sixty-one, but I'd worked hard to keep myself in shape and look as good as I could. But now, even my self-esteem in that area had worn thin.

I told him that I was losing my confidence in myself.

"I will leave then," he said

As soon as he said that, I blurted out, *"No, I don't want you to leave."* I couldn't imagine my life without him. I would face these fears and insecurities and get through them once and for all. I calmed down.

I could see that my ego *wanted* to be afraid, to fight for its identity—it felt lost, alone, abandoned and invisible when he was cold and critical—all of the wounds from my relationship with my mother. And yet, when he was like that, *he* was just afraid. And there we were, two people, lost and alone and separate, instead of warm and close.

We were finding our way through this morass and jungle of our minds' encasement of our hearts. Both of us had avoided loving deeply and completely and the freedom, depth and love available through our heart connection terrified our minds.

I remembered being seen and loved by my father and my sister. I could see now that I had to have that same relationship with myself—whole and complete within myself first and then sharing that with another.

And Landon and I both needed to have our clear, distinct wholeness, so we could hold the moments of deep and powerful oneness. I didn't know how to do that. Neither did he. But we were on this adventure together to discover how to live a real, alive, awake life, in duo.

"Hold on," the voice said. *"Hold on."*

"Bring it on—let's get through all of this," it said. Could I be strong enough to hold it that way?

We had a powerful talk and it felt good again. *"It's almost like deep sex when we talk and resolve things like that. So deep, so rich,"* I told him.

"I'm glad I'm doing this with you," he said.

I had some days alone and used that time to write and to reread a lot of what had happened in our relationship. That fed me somehow, to see how I had stayed true to myself and had stood strong against his mind, so many times.

During those days, something healed and some piece of the "not good enough" fell away. I knew he'd be crazy not to be with me—I am an amazing woman. That statement did not come from my ego, but from a deep sense of knowing who I am and what I came here to be—a deep, awake space of love and aliveness. And having him as my partner represented a big piece of that.

When he came back, as we made love in front of the fire, he seemed especially open and loving. He looked into my eyes and touched my face. *"Diane, you are so beautiful,"* he said. *"So beautiful,"* he said again. I breathed in his words and his love.

Later, I had to wonder, which came first—did I have to feel my own beauty inside for him to see it? It feels like I did. The new wholeness felt like a "clunk," an easing back in from having been just a few centimeters off from myself, but those centimeters meant everything.

I woke up with the voice saying, *"Say yes to love, laughter, light, and life."* I told Landon and he added *"and Landon."* I also added *"and lavish abundance."* We laughed. Things were light, stable and deep with us. As I continued to feel strong within myself, my relationship with him reflected that back.

Landon ⌒

About this time I started to see the simultaneity of upsets. It had to do with the fact that everything that exists, exists Now. In other words, even when I was not overtly experiencing an upset, or it was not acting out with sufficient force for me to notice it, that upset was operating as an undercurrent in my personality and some part of my life energy was playing through that pattern.

The second aspect, expressed by the *law of attraction,* states "we will always draw to us that which is in vibrational or energetic harmony with our own vibration." As both Diane and I worked on similar patterns of "not good enough," they would manifest in slightly different ways, but were the same at the core. I also realized that I had often denied my similar pattern in the past.

For example in a previous relationship, my partner had an obvious abandonment issue that led to her running away into the night or to binge eating and then days of excessive exercise.

I was not very understanding or compassionate and denied that I had any issue with separation and lack of connection. I even claimed to have dealt with it through the pain of my divorce, so I played the role of "I have it together and you are the problem."

Only later did I see that I too had been dealing with the same painful wound in a slightly different form. She and I could have healed that wound for both of us, if I had been willing to look and stay awake to myself. But at the time I did not understand the law of attraction as I do now, nor was I willing to look that deeply into myself.

With Diane, I also learned that as we gained more insight into our own minds' mechanisms and consequently experienced more freedom, the depth of our lovemaking and the ease of being together only got better. I was freer to be myself, "living out loud" so to speak, transparent and authentic, with this person to whom I was deeply connected. What a joy!

Diane ⌒

Right after Christmas, Landon was leaving for New Zealand for a month. I had been scheduled to go with him, but my daughter had her second child six weeks early, so I stayed behind to help her. The night before he left, we spent a romantic night at a bed and breakfast near San Francisco. *"I adore you and I'm so happy,"* he said. I was too.

The next morning, we went shopping, using the Nordstrom's gift card he'd given me for Christmas and he sat and waited while I tried things on. It was the first time I'd ever gone shopping with a man and I felt a little shy, but was so touched by his interest and help. Then it was time to say goodbye.

We weren't sure how long he'd be gone and my mind worried that he'd withdraw again. But I received a sweet email from him after he landed.

"Don't worry about us. Our relationship is too valuable and precious for me to do anything that might harm it. I miss you and love you. Landon."

Back at the farm, winter arrived in force, with snow and cold. I kept waking up in the middle of the night, feeling his energy, like we were linked up on the astral plane. I'd fall back asleep, loving him across the planet.

In the days just before the new year, as the snow fell outside, I sat by a crackling fire and took the time to be quiet and write about the new year ahead and also to look back on the year that was ending. We had moved through so many spaces since he had come one year before, and so much had healed.

We stayed close with calls and *Skype* as the days and weeks passed in the New Year and our love felt strong and stable.

I wrote, *"With Landon, how deep can we go and how much light can we hold?"* He was coming back at the end of four weeks and we could begin to discover the answers to those questions, together.

Chapter 13

The Light of My Heart

"We should never give up on our dreams of wholeness within ourselves and of wholeness with another."

- Diane's journal

Diane ⌒

We were both counting the hours till he came back from New Zealand. I cleaned and cleared, as I always did, wanting to create as much space as I could.

He arrived tired and we slept by the fire. *"You are precious to me,"* he said. That made me smile and snuggle into his strong arms again.

I could feel a whole, healed self, standing next to me now, strong, clear and beautiful. *"Don't do that, don't go there,"* it would say, if I started to get hooked by thoughts linked to pain. I could see the thoughts coming at me like the scenes in Mr. Toad's Wild Ride at Disneyland—crazy and out of control or sneaky and subtle. But now there was a second or even a millisecond pause, a moment to choose whether or not I got hooked.

He'd left before the New Year and now it was the last day of January. We had four days alone together, a deep, rich time to reconnect and create the year ahead.

Something basic to my soul felt fed now and fulfilled. It was something I'd waited lifetimes to have and yet recognized as familiar.

As we talked about the New Year, he offered to support me in my writing so that I could complete my memoir. *"That's nice,"* I said, thinking he meant "support," as in "encourage."

"No, I mean I want to financially support you in your writing," he said.

"Oh, wow." I was stunned.

I'd been doing it all myself for over thirty years. And writing had always had to take a back seat to paying the mortgage, the gas and light bill, and the phone bill. Yet when he offered, it took me so by surprise. As I let it sink in, it also brought up some fear of losing my independence—such an example of how the mind can make a problem out of anything! We talked about it and I told him all my fears, a good, authentic and powerful talk. I felt embarrassed to admit that I had those reservations.

"When you talk to me like this, I love you the most," he said.

We meditated together in the mornings and made love at night, both experiences of a space of bliss that we generated together, awake and alive, with no mind.

"I wish we were twenty and twenty-six," I told him. *"Then we'd have forty years of this experience."*

"We couldn't have had it then," he said. He was probably right.

On Valentine's Day, we went out to the *New Moon*, the restaurant we went to that first night, when he came up to talk about the book. The year before, I had flown over Valentine's Day on my way to New Zealand, skipping it entirely because of the International Date Line—an omen to the challenges I was going to face when I landed! But this year, we had a romantic dinner and then spent the evening making love by the fire. All the truth telling, strength and tenderhearted opening of the last year had been so worth it.

We had three good weeks together before he left to spend two and a half weeks with his mother, back east. While he was gone, I got snowed in with no power or water, no phone or Internet, for three days. I so missed, his warmth, his presence and his masculine strength as I crunched across the frozen ground to the woodshed to haul in the firewood and tried to stay warm, reading by the dim light of candles and gas lamps.

Having that quiet time alone gave me more perspective on my life and on our relationship. I wrote in my journal, *I fell in love at the unlikely age of sixty, unlikely in most 'mass consciousness' scenarios—too old, too late, too something. But I now know that we should never give up on our dreams of wholeness within ourselves and of wholeness with another.*

As I completed writing my memoir, some of the pain from my childhood began to feel more complete and healed. I could identify the chain of "not good enough" that had been passed down through the generations. My grandmother decided she wasn't good enough or my grandfather wouldn't have deserted her. My mother grew up under that shadow and knew she must not be good enough because her father had left them. I took it on, not only from their modeling, but from my mother's abuse.

My mother and grandmother never talked about this, but now I could see it all.

I felt more open, unafraid and present and my connection to Landon reflected those shifts. I needed less from him and felt strong, no matter what he did. And yet he gave me so much.

"I love how you stand up to me and how strong you are. You are so kind, loving and supportive, open to listening and changing your view. And so beautiful, prettier and prettier all the time," he said as we shared a powerful and intimate time by the fire.

A few days later, we left for New Zealand. When we landed in Auckland, I used my Australian passport, going through the line with Landon for Australian and New Zealand citizens. That felt amazing.

As we settled in, he became stressed about a real estate project he had there and became cold and withdrawn, the thing that always hooked me in my wounds of being misunderstood, invisible and abandoned. Maybe it was the jet lag and being so far from home, but it got to me and I told him.

He listened and was patient, seeing that I was in pain, and we healed it. I had to notice how far we'd come since the last trip there. I was learning to trust. If he withdrew, he just needed space and he would come back. He loved me.

Landon ⌒

I (and maybe all men) tend to focus on one thing at a time to the exclusion of all else. So back in New Zealand, as I worried about my real estate project and tried to figure out what to do, I just wanted to be left alone to concentrate. My withdrawal at that point had nothing to do with Diane even though it might have looked similar to times in the past when it was about her.

The fault on my part, if any, was that I did not communicate my worries and request the time to sort them out, telling Diane, "This has nothing to do with you." I was learning to be more skillful in that arena.

Diane ⌒

It felt like a blessing to be back at his beautiful home, to have the gift of time to write, with the ocean below, the sound of the waves, the sun, the clouds, and the rich smell of the green earth on the hills behind the house. I let it all feed me with its joy. Landon said he could feel it when I felt happy and free and it felt so good to him. That was cool—my joy fed us both.

I went down to the ocean and swam, floated and paddled, feeling energized and renewed and celebrating being back in New Zealand with him in our new life.

But as we prepared to go to Australia, I felt on edge. Was I really going back to where my mother came from, the place that had shaped her to be who she was and the country where the back-story of my life had taken place, where all the "not good enough" began? Should I even be going? Landon was a bit grumpy too, maybe affected by my emotions.

On the plane, I filled out the customs card and on the line where it said "citizenship," when I wrote "Australian," I had to blink and remind myself that it was true. At my turn at the custom's window, the woman looked at my passport photo, looked at me, stamped it and waved me on. I was an official Australian in Australia.

My cousin Brian and his wife welcomed us like long, lost family. Brian looked a lot like my brothers and felt like family from the first moment. His wife had prepared an elegant four-course dinner, served on English bone china dishes, with a linen tablecloth and napkins, so reminiscent of how my mother loved to serve meals.

The next day, we toured around Melbourne with Brian as our guide, stopping where my mother and her grandparents had lived, and visiting the site of one my great-grandfather's factories.

I climbed the steps and walked the halls of the historic town hall where my great-grandfather was mayor in 1900 and a councilman for many years, an impressive building with a clock tower. We searched through the Brighton cemetery in a light rain to find his grave, marked by a tall, white marble Celtic cross. *Michael Thomas Gleeson, 1846-1927.* I had never seen one of my ancestor's graves.

I was standing where my relatives had stood, the day of his burial, when they said goodbye to him. I touched his headstone and silently thanked him for taking care of my mother—her life would have been so much worse if he had not been waiting in the wings when her father left.

We walked through the crowded cobblestone alleyways in downtown Melbourne, crammed with sidewalk cafes. My relatives had walked those very streets. As we rode the tram around the city, I remembered stories my mother had told of taking the tram with her mother.

Melbourne's vibrant and bustling energy felt very European, lovely old buildings next to stark skyscrapers, the Yarra River winding through, the ocean just beyond. I loved having a link to this exciting city, to have history there that dated back to the 1850's when the family emigrated from Ireland. Thanks to my cousin Brian, the historian, I had all the rich details of the story.

I felt proud to be both American and Australian. It made me think of my parents and to cherish the different gifts they gave me. My father's love and acceptance gave me a strong foundation. But the pain that I experienced in my relationship with my mother took me deeper into life than I might have gone without it. It drove me to do the *est* training, for one thing, my link to Landon.

But the most powerful gift of the trip was that I could face the future, with a new peace about my past. My relationship with Landon felt strong and loving. Because I was now also an Australian citizen, I could come and go out of New Zealand, staying as long as I wanted. I looked forward to exploring Australia again and getting better acquainted with my new cousins and my new country.

Those are gifts my mother gave me. I could thank her for that.

We flew back to New Zealand and camped one night in Kaikora on the long drive home. We were both tired from the trip—that seems to bring things up. Landon went through another bout of "I wasn't his pictures."

It came out of the blue—he told me as we were sitting in a crowded restaurant, waiting for our dinner. We had been doing so well. I felt stunned and started to cry, surrounded by people.

"People are staring at me—they think this is reality TV," I said, but couldn't stop the tears from falling. I couldn't eat my dinner. He felt bad, but I felt worse, beaten down and discouraged. *How*

could I ever weather these storms with this man and would they never end?

I wanted to crawl away into a cave and hide. We slept in the van, on the beach, under a full moon. It could have been so romantic.

Landon ⌒

As we were leaving Melbourne and trying to return our rental car to catch our flight, we got lost. We were running out of time before our flight and Diane kept asking me to stop and ask for directions, which I resisted. The tension between us exacerbated the stress I felt and though we found the rental agency and made our flight, I continued to be grumpy, upset and angry at Diane for what felt like her criticism. What I said at dinner that night in Kaikora about how Diane didn't fit my pictures was my way of irresponsibly discharging some of the anger and upset I was still feeling.

Most of my life, I have been very sensitive to the upsets of my partners, starting with my mother, and have always tried to do something to fix the upsets. If my partner was upset, I thought it meant that I was not doing something right and therefore, I was "not good enough." Rather than acknowledge my own hurt feelings, I would suppress both the hurt and the anger that covered the hurt and then resent my partner for having to change to satisfy her.

This level of my pattern was surfacing, old wounds, old resentments, old behaviors of hiding what I was feeling and then discharging the anger in some irresponsible dumping of my feelings on my partner, or suppressing the anger to become more pain in my body.

I felt sad that I had hurt Diane, but I was not sufficiently on top of what was happening to do much else but say what was on my mind. Only in reflection am I now able to see what was going on.

Luckily, my strong angel Diane weathered this storm and when we once again talked it through, we were able to arrive at some peace.

Diane ⌒

The next morning, after that difficult night, he acted warm and loving. But I still felt wary. All my trust issues were up again. Somehow we got through that and got close again. Back at his house, I picked up one of his books on relationships and turned to a section about "fusers and isolators." Wow, did that fit. I was a "fuser," wanting to connect, and he was an "isolator," wanting to disconnect.

Just reading that there were other couples out there with the same issues helped. We talked about it and I realized that we were both making progress moving more towards the middle—I was becoming less needy and he was withdrawing less.

I was leaving New Zealand a week ahead of Landon, and as we sat in the airport waiting for my flight, I saw a woman who I had a hunch would be his "pictures." So I asked him, *"Is she it?"*

He looked and laughed, *"Yeah, she would be it."* She was about forty-five, blonde and skinny and was with a man, who was either her son or her boyfriend. But the great part was that it wasn't upsetting—it was rather funny that I could spot her. We talked about it as we snuggled close together in the hard plastic airport chairs before we had to say goodbye.

"Well, she's with another man, so you'd have to get through that barrier," I said, and we laughed. We had a loving goodbye and this time I knew I'd be coming back to New Zealand.

I arrived home, to the soft air of spring. My apple trees shimmered with pink and white blossoms, the grass was like a thick, green carpet and the bees buzzed busily. Landon came back a week later, and we relished sleeping out on the deck together, counting the stars in the clear skies as we fell asleep, warm under the covers in the chilly, spring night air.

Chapter 14

Counting Blessings

When I count my blessings, I count you twice.

- Irish Blessing

Diane ⌒

In June, we attended Landon's 50th high school reunion in Andover, Massachusetts. He seemed happy to introduce me as his partner to all his old friends.

"How could I have not seen how beautiful you are?" he asked.

"You had a cloud of fear over your eyes," I said, putting my hand over his eyes. He was being who and what I'd always known he could be. I was so grateful I'd stuck it out through the hard places.

Two weeks later, we left for three weeks in England and France. After he competed in a rowing regatta in Henley, England and won, we traveled to France for ten days of bicycling in the Alps.

I had booked us a room in a family run hotel in Annecy, near the border with Switzerland. We took the fast train across France, enjoying the fun of sitting back and relaxing while we sped across the countryside.

Our tiny room had a balcony overlooking the sparkling blue lake. We rented bikes and each day, after breakfast, we'd head out for a two-hour or longer bike ride. He tackled the challenging hills, some of which had been stages of the Tour de France. I pedaled around the lake, fairly flat and lovely, though I did venture out on harder rides as the days went on.

Evenings, we'd saunter down to the terrace for dinner. By the end of our visit, we felt like a part of the family, with the staff and owners. I so loved speaking French again and sharing the beauty of France with him. I had visited Annecy almost thirty years before and promised myself that I would come back some day. I relished fulfilling that dream with him.

We arrived back home from France to summer, sleeping outside, going to the river, and enjoying the long warm days. The first time he got moody and withdrew, I went outside and dug in the garden, something that always made me felt better and usually solved whatever I was brooding about.

What if I could just give him space to have his moods and not push him so hard to be an image of what I think he should be? That felt so important. He came back from rowing in a good mood, and put his arms around me, validating my new perspective. We were taking new ground and keeping it. After we attended the workshop "Acting for Non-Actors" in Montreal, he opened up even more. Life felt happy and good.

Landon ⌒

During our trip to England and France, we had dinner with my old boss from *est,* Werner Erhard and his wife Gonneke, in London. It was a great reunion after so many years and at the end of our visit, Werner invited Diane and me to attend his workshop in Montreal, *Acting for Non-Actors.* After we participated in that workshop in August 2011, we both felt re-inspired to create a more conscious future, a new "third act" in our life.

Shortly after the workshop, I finally saw my "this isn't it" as a pattern that I could choose to follow or that I could withdraw my life energy from. It was no longer some given fact for me, or the undercurrent of my life, but had become identified for what it was, FEAR—*False Evidence Appearing Real.*

As I opened up to living in "this is it" rather than the opposite, the positive effects reverberated through my life. I felt centered, whole and satisfied to my core. In this new and different experience, my lesser patterns like "not good enough" or fears or resistances to life as it is just seemed to fade away as soon as I recognized them.

I was more able to maintain Diane's and my connection without retreating into "being separate and alone" after our intense lovemaking. All in all, life took on a new shine.

Diane ⌒

After the workshop in Montreal, we had several deep and stable weeks of connection and then he left for a quick two-week trip to New Zealand. I thought of how my grandmother used to take weeks to travel by ship to Australia. And now the journey took just twelve hours.

I remembered how the psychic saw "Big Love" over two and a half years before—and she was so right. We'd been opening up to falling in love, not based on a fantasy, but on a solid foundation of telling the truth and staying awake. We couldn't lose that.

"You were made for me," he said as we said a tender goodbye. Two weeks apart I could stand. We'd still have the river when he came back, and the cabin at the lake for five days. We had come so far and it felt like this time, we didn't have to go back.

During the two weeks, we kept a rich connection through emails, phone calls and *Skype.* I woke up the day of his return, thinking of him flying through the sky. As I lay in bed, feeling the excitement of that, I thought of my mother and wrote in my journal, *"My mother did the best she could. And somewhere, out in the universe, she rests easier because I know that."*

That day, my friend Sarah and I scurried around, cleaning and creating space. The house sparkled, I put clean sheets on the bed, picked fresh flowers, washed my hair, even cleaned the clutter off my desk. It felt as big as the first time he had come and then that first weekend when he came back. I even wondered, *maybe he's going to ask me to marry him?* But then I let that go. I didn't want to set up an expectation.

The voice came back—I hadn't heard it in a while.

"The energy is big. It's going to feel like flying through space without a space ship, at times. You've been doing well on your own. But it is big now."

He pulled in about five in the evening. It felt so luscious to be in his arms again and to have him home. We chatted and laughed, so happy to be together again.

I'd made his favorite dinner of salmon, salad and fresh vegetables and had the table set out on the deck, with sunflowers from the garden and soft candlelight. As we got ready to eat, he said he'd have a glass of wine. That got my attention—he rarely drank wine. I got out two crystal glasses and we had a lovely toast, making the glasses chime, before we sipped the wine.

As we sat at the table and did our usual hand squeeze, looking into each other's eyes for a moment of gratitude, he looked around at the farm, the huge oak tree, the evening sky, then back at me, with warmth and love in his eyes.

"This is so great. I'm so glad to be back. You look beautiful."

"Thank you." I smiled at him, then picked up my fork to start to eat.

"What do you think about marrying me?" he asked.

"What did you say?" I put down my fork, my eyes wide.

"I said, 'What do you think about marrying me—it isn't a proposal.'"

"Okay, let's talk about it not being a proposal..." I answered, looking at him sideways, a little confused.

He smiled. We looked at each other. He took my hand.

"Will you marry me?" he asked.

"Will you ask me again?" I stammered, not quite believing my ears.

"Diane, will you marry me?"

"Yes, I will marry you Landon." I laughed and cried, not able to eat a bite of dinner.

We slept out under the stars, feeling the joy of being back together, in body, mind and spirit and relishing our new, big milestone.

Landon ⌣⁓

I had thought about marriage in the past, and Diane and I had even talked about the "M" word some time back, just to get the charge off the word so it could be brought up in conversation in a more neutral way. I was only willing to commit to a partner who was strong enough to meet me at the deepest levels and to go toe to toe with me on this road to full enlightenment. After two years of being together, I knew I had found that partner in Diane. And I was conquering the old programming and seeing Diane as radiantly beautiful more and more often. Finally all the pieces were coming together.

Also during the summer of 2011, whenever I had doubts about Diane, I would say to myself, *"Okay if you leave Diane, who would you like to be with and what life would you like to have?"* The answer was always, *"Diane and the life we have."* So I was kind of surrounded by Diane, giving a new meaning to the word "trapped" as this time, I was trapped in what I wanted!

In New Zealand, away from Diane and consumed with my real estate project that had gone to Environment Court, I realized I did not want to live the rest of my life without her. But as I returned to our home, I had not planned to ask her to marry me—I didn't have a ring or even a bouquet of flowers!

As we sat down to dinner on our deck underneath the giant oak tree, with the sun setting and two candles flickering on the table framing Diane's lovely face, I took her hands in mine and looked into her clear blue eyes to say our customary blessing.

At that moment, I knew that she was "it" for me. In a kind of hesitant voice I asked her what she thought about marriage?

When she responded, *"Is that a proposal?"* I took the leap and said from the depths of my being, *"Will you marry me, my darling Diane?"* I felt certain at last.

Diane ⌒

The ring...

All through my life, my mother spoke of her grandfather, Michael Thomas Gleeson, with awe. How he was a powerful politician in North Melbourne, rich, successful and the father of thirteen children, nine with his first wife and four with his second, my great-grandmother Catherine Bridget Gleeson.

My great-grandfather had a diamond ring in a wide gold band; the ring was unusual, because the diamond could be unscrewed and then screwed back into a tie tack. I heard about the diamond ring/tie-tack when my mother told us stories about Australia that were a part of the backdrop of my childhood.

My mother returned to Australia only a few times and fell out with the maiden aunt who inherited all the family wealth and treasures. So when this Aunt died, the ring/tie-tack ended up being given to the Catholic Church. My mother tracked it down and bought it back for three thousand dollars in the late 1980's.

I saw the ring a few times when my mother wore it, and felt the energy that it carried, of this man and this place I was connected to, so far across the planet and so long ago.

When my mother died, I knew I had to have that ring. I had to buy it from the estate, three thousand dollars again, a lot of money at the time, but there was no question about it. I wasn't consciously thinking of how I would use it or wear it, I just knew it was mine to have and to keep.

Now, as I type this, the diamond sparkles on my left hand, surrounded by two bright blue sapphires on a slim white gold band, my engagement ring with Landon. It feels right to be wearing something precious of my great-grandfather's, from the late 1800's, a link from a good man, through over a century of troubles and turmoil, to a time of love and peace again.

My mind hasn't always understood the pressing need I've felt to unravel the pain and try to heal the broken places in my life. But I have *trusted* the necessity of it, the pulls, nudges and even kicks by the universe as I've moved along my path through life.

And now, waking up out under the huge oak trees, in the arms of my beloved Landon, I can feel that the stories are grateful, the characters in them are grateful and their souls rest easier, wherever they are. They know that one person unraveled it all and wove together a life out of what had seemed like shredded fragments.

There is a strength and a wholeness in the fabric of my life now, and the rich bright colors of love, peace, and joy. I am so grateful.

Chapter 15

The Wedding

"My search for a partner has ended.
I feel whole and complete..."

- Landon, at the wedding

Landon ⌒

After Diane agreed to marry me, I felt a deep sense of satisfaction that I had finally completed a long standing, unresolved aspect of my life. I felt grounded and at home on our farm, with its fruit trees, chickens, cats and all, and with the perfect person for me. I couldn't be happier. Even the little irritations just seemed to arise and pass away in the space of our love and the pleasure just kept getting better.

Starting in November, we remodeled the farm's old, small, dark kitchen. A wall came down to open up space and let in light. Green linoleum counter tops and dark wood cabinets transformed to a granite island and white cupboards, with large new windows filling the room with light. It changed the whole living dynamics of the house as we now spent almost all our time in this beautiful space that included a wood stove and my desk.

Surprising us both, we did not argue once during the two-month remodel and made all the decisions and choices easily together—sinks, flooring, windows, counter tops—we liked the same things. I saw that as a great validation of the lack of upset in our relationship. Also, it was our first real creation together and it felt good that we could do something of that magnitude and have it go smoothly.

One night lying in bed, six-weeks before the wedding date, I suggested that we use the wedding as an opportunity to complete everything in our lives that was not complete, so that the wedding was actually an acknowledgement of not only our relationship but also a foundation for whatever was next.

For me, this included clearing up some things with one of my children, completely revamping the wood shed by splitting and restacking all the wood, remodeling the old goat shed into an exercise room and spare bedroom, turning another shed into a meditation room, building a tool shed for the garden, and making paths to the creek in the woods.

I had planned on inviting all my old friends and I wanted them to have a great time and also experience the magic of our farm. I was proud to be a part of Diane's world and I wanted to contribute to it in every way I could.

In addition to a quick trip to New Zealand to complete some business projects, the tasks listed above took a full time effort the rest of that spring. Finally a week before the wedding, I could say that everything was complete on the farm.

Diane had been managing all the wedding plans with my assistance and this too was finally complete just as my brother and his wife, the first of our one hundred plus guests, arrived at our house from Denmark.

One of the things that I was a little nervous about was whether I would be able to be authentic and present on our wedding day. I knew I loved Diane, but would I be able to really show her how much I loved her in front of so many people? For weeks I wrote and re-wrote what I was going to say to our assembled friends by way of introduction and our vows to each other. I had planned on really learning my lines and with all my experience of being in front of a room full of people, I was sure I could accomplish that.

Days passed and the events of the wedding progressed— friends arriving and being shown around the farm, a bachelor night with about sixteen men where we drank Drambuie and discussed what it means to be a man at this time in history and at our respective ages. Then there were tables and chairs to be set up, the arrangement of the wedding alcove, the rehearsal dinner, and many more details that "only I could handle." All of a sudden I was taking a shower just before the ceremony and I still did not know my lines!

Luckily I had written them down and decided that I would use what I had written as needed. My two brothers and I walked to the front first and I welcomed our guests with the following:

Welcome, thank you for coming.

You are a large portion of our community of support, our friends and family, our chosen tribe. And I am so grateful that you are here, now, with Diane and me.

I first came into Diane's presence (at least consciously, that is) just as you did today, by driving up the driveway onto this beautiful property.

Many of you have known me for a long time and all of you have known me with some form of "This isn't it" playing through me and defining who I am. I have lived with an underlying "dissatisfaction" and a sense of "not being good enough" all my life.

So when I drove up the drive that day in October 2009, I was pretty burned out in the relationship department with a long record of failed attempts, a resigned attitude and little hope of ever finding "the one."

What took place was not my standard "fall in love" experience, in fact with Diane I have characterized it as "falling in love backwards."

I started liking the property (a reflection of Diane of course) and liking the reality of my experience with Diane, but she started where all others had ended, as just another, "this isn't it." From there it got both better and worse as different levels of the patterns we each carried into the relationship surfaced and got seen for what they were, mostly mistakes made by children.

The success of our relationship came from our commitment to telling the raw truth of our experience, our willingness to each look to ourselves as the source of the joint upset we were having and Diane's unrelenting commitment to something she could see when I could not.

And last but not least, my willingness to keep surrendering to the pleasure and ecstasy of Diane. I know that may not seem hard, but it was for me because I was holding on to "dear old ego" for all I was worth and resisting!

Through all of this, I gained an enormous respect for Diane, for her courage to stand up to me and to not give up on "us," although I sometimes pushed her to her limits. So Diane deserves all the credit for what we are celebrating today.

My college best friend, Mike Wick, who could not be here today, said "Diane saved your life" and he was right.

Diane is my Angel. Through her loving me, I have learned how to love myself. And in loving myself, I have been able to love Diane more deeply. I can now see her goodness, her kindness, her beauty, her huge heart and her courage in the path we have chosen.

I stand before you at this moment, totally fulfilled and wondering how I deserve such good fortune and I am grateful for you, my family and friends in our lives.

My search for a partner has ended, I feel whole and complete at the level of male/female connection. And I feel grounded and connected to this land and our living earth—as if I'm a channel between earth and sky.

I always wanted both freedom to be myself and true connection with another. Now I have both.

The following song "Go Where Love Goes" sung by Andrea Bocelli has been my guiding star since I heard it and certainly has brought me here to be with beautiful Diane.

After the song, my two lovely granddaughters, ages three and five, led the procession of grandchildren, followed by Diane's daughters. Then I looked across the audience and saw my gorgeous Diane, looking more radiant and beautiful than I had ever seen her.

My heart filled with love and gratitude. I felt totally fulfilled, whole, complete and satisfied, for certainly this must be heaven on earth to experience that much love. Along with the birth of my children, this will always be one of my most cherished memories.

During the moving ceremony, that followed we laughed and cried together. Many of our friends and family told us that they too were moved and experienced a new awakening and depth in their own relationships. We both felt the satisfaction of knowing that by being our authentic selves, our joy and love could make a powerful contribution to others.

Diane ⌒

I, who believe passionately in the power of words, have been afraid I could not find the right ones to do justice to the magic and perfection of our wondrous wedding day.

But I am going to have courage here and do my best to describe it.

First of all, people say that planning a wedding often creates stress for couples. Luckily, I'd planned events over the years as part of my various jobs, so didn't mind the challenges of organizing the big pieces of the puzzle—the food, chairs and tables, linens, flowers, music, lights, sound and all the little pieces in between that would make it elegant and beautiful.

I'd hoped to get it all done a week ahead, but that plan didn't materialize, so there were a few moments in the final days when I started to feel stressed. Then Landon stepped up and asked *"what can I do to help?"* and took over as many of the last minute details as he could, printing the programs, organizing helpers for set-up and doing the seating charts. That just made me love him more.

Our ceremony and reception were to be outside at the farm and people always asked us, *"What is your plan B in case it rains?"* We didn't have a plan B. So we hoped and prayed and then celebrated when the weather forecast predicted "sunny and mild."

For my wedding dress, I had wanted a long, light green silk dress, on the bias—I could see it in my mind. Landon and I went shopping and we found it at the first store we went to. It felt so feminine—clingy and lovely. All the other pieces fell into place just as easily—shoes, jewelry, "something old, something new, something borrowed, something blue."

On the morning of the wedding, I snuck off to my hairdresser and she did my hair with little crystals that matched the tiny crystals in the fabric of my dress. I felt like a fairy princess as I waited to walk out and greet my future husband.

The ceremony started in the late afternoon and friends and family came over in the morning to help with setting-up tables and chairs, arranging flowers, and all the last minute tasks that needed to be done.

At three-fifteen, the musicians, a harpist and violinist, began playing soft background music as the guests mingled before the ceremony. Our one-hundred guests, ranging in ages from three months to eighty-five, had come from as far away as Australia and the east coast of the US, excited to celebrate with us.

All the "little angels" as I called them—our grandchildren and my sister's two grandchildren, gathered in the house with me and my daughters, who were my bridesmaids. We would walk out after Landon greeted the guests and spoke.

Landon walked in with his brothers, then told everyone the story of our relationship—the "falling in love backwards." His voice broke and he cried a few times as he thanked me for being his angel and for hanging in there with him through all the tough times.

I sat on the deck and listened, wiping away my own tears, being so moved by his words. My grandson Hunter, aged four, asked with real concern, *"Why is grandma Diane crying?"* He didn't understand that someone could cry from being moved or from joy. Many of the guests cried too, as Landon shared with such genuine and deep openness. Landon then played his special song, "Go where love goes," sung by Andrea Bocelli.

The little angels, all dressed in white, walked out, two by two, scattering rose petals, as the musicians played, "Jesus Joy of Man's Desiring." There were eight of them, in all, with my eldest granddaughter, twelve, holding hands with and carrying my youngest granddaughter, eighteen months.

Then my beautiful daughters walked out, also dressed in white, to the strains of my sister Sharon's favorite song, "Wild Mountain Thyme." I chose it to include Sharon in our special day and to honor how her love had helped me and kept me strong through the hard times in my life. I so wished she could have been there that day to share in our joy.

As I walked out, I took a deep breath to let it all in—the blue sky and the tall trees and loveliness of the farm, the flowers on the tables, and all our special people gathered there, smiling at me. And Landon, in front waiting for me, surrounded by his brothers and my precious daughters and grand children. Everyone stood up as I walked along, following the rose petals.

When I turned at the aisle, I stopped and looked ahead at Landon, feeling the depth and the power of the step we were about to take together. It felt so right.

Landon greeted me with a kiss, then they all sat and I spoke, of my journey with the farm and how it had helped me to heal, and how I'd dreamed of sharing it with a partner one day. I shared two things that my sister had said to me, *"Someday someone is going to come along and see how big your heart is"* and, *"whoever you end up with, make sure he loves you and not just your farm."*

That got a big laugh, since Landon had just shared how he fell in love with the farm before he fell in love with me. *"But,"* I added, *"he didn't realize then that the farm and I were a package deal."* I then played "The Blessing," a song which reflected the tenderness of my love for Landon.

The psychic, Tantra Maat, who had predicted that "Big Love" was coming two and a half years earlier, was also a minister and performed the ceremony. That felt perfect, too.

We wrote our own vows but also decided to say the traditional vows at the end. Here are the vows I wrote and said to Landon:

Landon, I promise to love you,
to look for your goodness,
your strengths, and your greatness.
I promise to hold you in the warmth of my arms,
in good times and in hard times
and to look for the truth instead of trying to be right.

I promise to feel the joy and the gratitude
of sharing my life with you,
knowing that even the challenges are what I chose,
when I chose you.

I choose you as my partner, as my husband,
to grow with and learn with,
to laugh with and cry with
as we journey through the rest of our lives together.

And for the exchange of rings:
This ring represents my joining with you,
in the unbroken circle of our love.
May it remind us of the joy that we share
and of our commitment to each other,
to freedom
and to the truth.

I bless the day I found you
and I choose you,
with all of my heart,
as my husband and partner on this journey of life.

And the traditional vows:

I, Diane Mary Covington,
take you Charles Landon Carter
to be my husband.
I promise to stand beside you and with you always,
in times of celebration and in times of sorrow,
in sickness and in health.

I will live with you and love you,
as long as we both shall live.

When Tantra pronounced us "husband and wife" and introduced us as "Landon and Diane Carter," everyone cheered, including us.

Then the party began! We took family photos, toasted with champagne, had a scrumptious salmon and tri-tip dinner, topped off with carrot cake and strawberries dipped into chocolate. We were toasted and roasted, amid a lot of laughter, cheers and some tears.

We danced our first dance to "At Last," a song by Mack Gordon and Harry Warren. The words, *"At last, my love has come along, my lonely days are over and my life is like a song,"* felt so appropriate. We swayed and snuggled close, as friends circled around us and sang along.

We celebrated and partied under the Japanese lanterns strung overhead, to "oldies" and some of my granddaughters' "new" favorite music. Some guests wandered over to a crackling bonfire in the fire circle in the garden to mingle and talk.

As the party wound down, Landon and I snuck away to spend our wedding night at a friend's cottage out in the woods, with a bathtub for two, chocolate truffles and rose petals on the pillows. As we soaked, we relished how perfect the day had been—the food, the music, the guests, the ceremony, even the parking had all gone off without a hitch. We made love as husband and wife, both feeling the joy of our commitment and the excitement about the open future ahead of us.

The next morning, we returned home to find everything cleaned up and put away, a gift of friends who had helped out the night before. Family and out of town friends returned for a brunch, one last chance to connect and visit before everyone scattered again to return home.

When I had married forty-four years before, nineteen and pregnant, scared and uncertain, the priest had rushed through the ceremony and we had answered the questions, remote and stilted "I do." I had long since made peace with the fact that I didn't keep those vows. I was just too young!

This time, however, I almost shouted out the words "I Diane Mary Covington, take you Charles Landon Carter, to be my husband." It felt so powerful to be so certain. *This is what a wedding should feel like,* I thought, as the special day unfolded.

We set off on a road trip to the Pacific Northwest, with our bikes on the back of the van. For those two weeks, we savored being "newlyweds" on our honeymoon. I heard myself saying things like, *"my husband went to get the car"* and relished using that word as part of my vocabulary again. It *did* feel different, to know that we were married, that we had taken that step and made that commitment to each other.

Now, as Landon and I share our lives, as husband and wife, I feel profound gratitude for my life, for all of the joy and grounded happiness I feel living with my husband.

I know now, that, just like in the fairy tales, dreams really do come true. And I also know, for certain, that there *really* is such a thing as "happily ever after."

Diane's Epilogue

As you can see, we didn't start out with "happily ever after." We really did "fall in love backwards," at least *he* did, and because he was not in love with me, I had to hide the depth of my love for him, until he was ready to receive it.

But I did love him from the first time he came back into my life and that love kept me strong.

Courage comes from the root of "coeur" in French, "heart." *"Stay in your heart no matter what. That is where your wisdom lives and breathes,"* my inner voice said, over and over.

And I did. I stayed tender and open, and he said that saved it. No woman had ever been able to stay with him and not abandon him in his pain. I had never been able to stay tender and open in the midst of my pain with a man either. That took both courage and heart and I'm grateful for the Divine help I had to do that.

My inner guidance even told me on the first night of pain in New Zealand, *"We chose you to do this because you're the only person strong enough to be with him through it."*

Oh great, my mind said. *Thanks a lot.* And that's one of the miracles of the whole experience—that I could hear my mind—loud, rattled, cynical, and scared, repeating its favorite phrase *Run!* But the deeper, calm space knew exactly what to do—feel it all, and let it burn off all this old pain, heal the old wounds and open up to a new life.

I chose that voice, that energy, because I trusted that it was new. It calmed me and centered me, while the other voice made me want to scream and cry. It was clear which one to choose.

And yet it had taken me over sixty years to get to the place of being able to make that choice, of being able to hear that other voice. John O'Donohue taught me to treat myself with great tenderness. It took some time, but I learned to do that.

I had hardened my heart in my relationship with my mother. And I'm so grateful that it could "unharden," soften, open and stay open, even in the midst of the wounds from her—feeling invisible, misunderstood, not good enough, unloved. That's a piece of work that I can cherish and be proud of. I am proud that I trusted tenderness.

Over thirty years ago, when Landon told me to *"use everything you've got to make a difference in life,"* it changed the course of my life. Then thirty years later, it took all the skills, all the self-mastery I'd worked for, even undiscovered strength— *everything I had,* to stay with him through our challenging times. He helped me all those years ago, so that I could grow strong and come back around and help him, and help us. Life is filled with such magic and mystery.

The Shaman called out to the universe for a "true partner" for Landon and I answered, thinking of him within twenty-four hours of his healing. The universe sent me, but Landon tried to send me back! One night we laughed about the image of him trying to reject me and send me back. But I refused to be rejected, like the Bozo Doll that bounced back or the Terminator that kept on coming.

In the hard times in our relationship, it felt like I was in a trusty, little, wooden boat in very rough seas. My boat of *"what we have is real. There is real magic between us. Let's not waste this. This is precious,"* would be hit by a huge wave, quiver, go under, then bob back up. My love kept me afloat and now my little boat has transformed into a lovely and sturdy vessel that can weather any storms. She sails on calm seas, with bright and sunny days for laughter, fun, swimming and playing.

There's room on this boat for the two of us. So where are we going to take her? Where are we journeying to? We're both excited to create the answers to those questions together.

And now my own personal pointers on finding a partner, growing together and staying strong through the rough seas that can come up, so you sail out the other side into happiness and bliss.

First of all, if you're looking for a relationship, do some preparation work to be ready and able to attract a healthy partner. Get some help to heal your childhood wounds. There are so many good programs out there—Landmark Education, for example, or other weekend seminars which can give you a new perspective on life. Or find a good therapist and get to work. Open your mind, get some help, do your best to heal and be willing to let go of your past and move forward. Your life is waiting for you.

Develop your relationship skills. Learn to listen well. Excellent communication is the foundation for a healthy relationship that can weather the storms. As a life coach, when couples come to me for help, I teach them how to listen to each other without reacting or thinking ahead to how they are going to respond. In other words, they learn to be a safe place for each other to express feelings without judgment.

They also learn not to blame each other, but to look at their own patterns and history to find the real source of the upset. With a foundation of good communication, each person can tell the truth and real intimacy and love can flourish.

Look for a partner who shares your deep values. That saves so much time and energy. Landon and I agree on our political views, our commitment to health, our love of nature, our relationship to spirituality and most of all, our commitment to living an awake life. We had been on similar, parallel paths and when those paths crossed, we had so much in common that it created a strong base to stand on to begin to deal with the deep issues that came up.

In real estate, when you buy a home, the owners have to do a "disclosure agreement" where they list what is wrong with the house. *"The roof leaks, or there is a crack in the foundation,"* for example. It would be great if two people starting out in relationship could do the same. Instead of trying to perpetuate the fantasy of being perfect, what if both people could tell the truth about their deep issues?

For example, *"I know I look strong, but you have to know that I feel not good enough, hate being misunderstood or feeling invisible."* If the other person did the same, then they would both have a clear idea about the booby traps of the mind they're navigating together. In order to do this, each person has to have identified what his or her issues are. Another reason to get to work on your personal growth.

What if you could welcome the "hot spots" where you're touchy and know, *here's an area to heal, wow, that means soon I'll be even happier and more free! And out of resolving it together, we'll be able to enjoy even deeper love and intimacy.* I know that may sound like a fantasy, but we've come to know that it is the truth.

If you're not sure what your "hot spots" are, just make a list of what you get "hooked by," upset about or get into arguments about. Then look and see what the underlying issues could be that you're protecting and that are as yet unhealed. The point is, to not run away from the hard places, but rather to know that they are the way out of the maze of pain and into the light and joy.

One last thought. I had something I'd created called a "desert island test" to know if a partner and I fit for a long-term commitment. Could I be on a desert island alone with him, no TV, no job titles, no bank accounts, just the two of us and a few palm trees?

Could I imagine myself happy with just this person? If I couldn't, then I knew he wasn't "the one" for me. Landon passed this test. From the very beginning, we spent most of our time alone together. Now we still do and love it.

As I look back to my childhood, I can see the little girl curled up with her fairy tale book, wondering if "happily ever after" really existed but longing to find it somehow.

I now know that "happily ever after" is about love so deep and vast and pure that it resonates with trees, rivers, moonlight, meteors and pure magic.

That's the kind of love I came here to have and that's what Landon and I now share. Almost three years ago, our relationship began out on the deck under the stars. The other night, we watched meteor showers as we lay out under the dark night sky. It's so powerful to see how far we've come and yet to be right where we began, snuggling together outside.

I offered to help Landon make his book stronger—to add more stories. So writing brought us together. Now we've co-authored this book, which reflects our distinct styles and personalities, that I believe combine to create a powerful whole.

It is my deepest wish that our book will help you to find your own true love, your own *"happily ever after."*

Landon's Epilogue

Shared Intimacy as a Path to Enlightenment

I have practiced many different paths that claim to lead to enlightenment, sitting by myself for days on end, writing all my thoughts until there was nothing left to write, ten-day silent Buddhist vipassana meditation retreats, living in an ashram in India, pranayama, yoga asanas, chanting, mantras, fasting, etc.

Now, I am a firm believer that shared intimacy with a committed partner, is perhaps one of the fastest and most efficient methods of gaining freedom from the upsets that take us away from Being, Here, Now and having the life we want.

There are examples of exalted relationships even in the ancient eastern tradition where the whole notion of enlightenment was born, Shiva and Shakti and Rama and Sita. But there is little information about what it took to make them great examples of the union of God/Goddess or male/female energies.

I am reminded of the story of the revered guru who spent most of his life meditating in a cave and people would come to him for answers to their deepest questions. One day he left his cave and went to the market where someone jostled him and he got angry. So much for being free!

The point is that in the cave, he never had to confront that aspect of himself, so when the situation arose in the market that triggered that pattern, he got upset. And in that moment, the upset was controlling him, not his free choice.

One of the beneficial aspects of an intimate relationship, is that the more you open up and the more vulnerable you become, the core patterns and programming that prevent you from Being your free and unencumbered Self will surface to be dealt with and healed.

The reward for dealing with that next deeper level of upset is more joy, ecstasy, connection and trust, which in turn becomes the foundation for dealing with the next level or what ever programming is left. In the meantime, there is more freedom to be your Self and to choose how to Be or "show up" in any given situation.

This has certainly been true with Diane and me, as I hope our story has shown. However, since you will not be sitting with an enlightened master who supposedly knows what is best for your next step, you will need some agreements that you are committed to in order to set up the conditions for this enlightenment path to work.

As two awake individuals who had done lots of work on ourselves and worked with thousands of others, we still had plenty of dysfunctional programming and baggage that we brought with us into the relationship. It was the following orientation and agreements that helped us through the morass of our own ego minds.

The first is that you are more committed to Freedom from the upsets that subvert your happiness and well being than you are to being comfortable or being right about your view. It is only this commitment to Enlightenment and Freedom that will give you the incentive and courage to confront the issues and tell the truth about them, rather than to come to some comfortable compromise or tacit agreement that "we just won't talk about that."

The second is a commitment to being awake to yourself, to "seeing yourself in action" whenever possible and an orientation of personal responsibility for your own experience, especially when you are upset. This means looking for and acknowledging your own body sensations, feelings, thoughts, decisions, beliefs and earlier similar incidents from your past that are related to the current upset.

To do this work you will need an understanding or model of the Observer Self, how the mind is structured, and how the primitive survival mechanisms and the filters of perception play havoc with your life. Also, the dynamics of the right/wrong game, the nature of upsets, how the ego is structured and some of the core tenets of your personality.

All of these topics and more have been covered in my previous book, *Living Awake*. It works better if both partners have a common understanding of the metaphysical model within which they are operating, but it is not entirely necessary.

The third is an agreement to not blame your partner for your upsets. This requires an understanding that upsets are triggered and not caused by your partner or the current circumstances, but that they are a replay of some earlier similar trauma, usually from early childhood. And therefore, all your thoughts, feelings, body sensations and actions are programmed and driven by this earlier event (that you survived) and are now replaying at some level of intensity.

The fourth is a commitment to be authentic and tell the raw, uncensored truth of your experience—your thoughts, emotions, beliefs, etc.

The fifth is to listen to your partner's experience and to hold it with the same validity as you hold your own experience. If you truly listen without resistance and "get" the communication (some people say "recreate the other's communication") the charge will start to lessen for your partner and what is being said will move into a neutral condition of simply being information— no resistance, no defensiveness on your part.

It's important to learn how to listen without defensiveness for this process to work. Most people think that listening means they are agreeing to what the other is saying, but it doesn't. You are just getting that what he/she is saying is true, over there, in his/her experience. After you have listened to your partner's words, and acknowledged hearing them, then you can say your side. Back and forth, really hearing each other, can begin to heal the issue.

The sixth is to be responsible for your own happiness and to let go of being upset as soon as you are able. This manifests your commitment to having love and happiness over your mind's addiction to being right and dissatisfied.

In addition, setting time frames within which you can go for it one hundred percent seemed to work well for Diane and me. "The nineteen-day experiment," and "the seven-month adventure of falling in love" and "the four months until her birthday," gave us time where the mind was held in abeyance and we could simply live and interact together, without the constant pressure of "do we continue or not?"

And I believe seeking help from a therapist oriented around you being one hundred percent responsible for your experience, or talking to a centered friend, or journaling as Diane does, are useful. They allow you to get some perspective on what your mind is bringing up so that you can observe it with more clarity and neutrality.

And finally, *don't resist being upset*, as that is always the starting point for the conversation and inquiry that follow. The upset is the indication that there is something to work on and is the opportunity to go through another door to expansion and freedom. Be thankful for your upsets, they are the way out!

An example of this process: I had always heard that you needed to love yourself first before you could love others. And that self-love was a foundation for generosity, gratitude and compassion. However in all my years, my mostly unexamined "not good enough" robbed me of the experience of total self-acceptance and self-love. No amount of other practices seemed to get to the issues that prevented me from loving myself.

Only through this process and Diane loving me with the fierceness that she demonstrated and accepting me the way I am, allowed me to expand my capacity to accept and love myself. Loving myself more allowed me to love Diane more, which I desired and which she deserved.

It has been a mutual opening up and letting go into love as more and more of the patterns have discharged. And for this I am eternally grateful to my wonderful partner and now wife, Diane.

A final note: the inquiry I started about the nature of love has resolved itself for me in the following way. I now see love as formless, a declared empty space, created with the words "I love you," that accepts the other person without reservation. A space within which all emotions are accepted and none are indications of whether I love this person or not.

It seems to parallel a similar acceptance of myself, for if I can't give love to myself how can I extend it to another? It also seems to be accompanied by an unreserved intention for my partner's well being and happiness, in the same way that I intend the best for myself.

Within this empty space of love, I am free to create the form of love I most desire, to have the time of my life—romance, fun, passion, deep conversations, shared quiet, exhilarating joint creations—fill in the blanks. The desire to have this life of love and fulfillment that we all so deserve, now becomes the motivator to clear the space of all the upsets that inhibit our ability to BE HAPPY.

We wish you all the very best on your journey.

About
Diane Covington-Carter and Landon Carter

Diane Covington-Carter graduated with honors from UCLA and has received awards for her writing, photography and NPR commentaries. She has been a life coach for over thirty years, on a quest to discover the truth about the mysteries of happiness and love, both for herself and others.

For over forty years, Landon Carter has dedicated his life to learning about and understanding how we create reality and to sharing those insights. A graduate of Andover, Yale and Harvard Business school, he has been a trainer with *est* (now Landmark Education) and several other human potential and business seminars.

Landon and Diane lead seminars and work with individuals and couples internationally. They live in Northern California and New Zealand.

For more information visit

www.fallinginlovebackwards.com

Made in the USA
Lexington, KY
14 July 2014